OLD PATTERN GLASS
ACCORDING TO HEACOCK

by
William Heacock

Featuring the early columns of William Heacock
(1974 to 1980)

For Mom
To Scorpio From Leo

TABLE OF CONTENTS

INTRODUCTION

As a man of few words I was quite surprised there were so many when I gathered together the columns I wrote from 1974 to 1980. These originally appeared in the periodicals *Antique Trader Weekly* and the monthly *Glass Review* magazine. The past five years have literally disappeared in a glimpse, but this book brought it all back to me. Each column recalled a special memory, a moment of pleasure or struggle, the ups and the downs of a fascinating career.

From the earliest column to the latest, my writing style has changed very little. I still apologize too much, present my thoughts unclearly, and construct sentences worthy of a Pulitzer Prize for sheer length. I think of myself as a researcher who must publish his findings. How I present them may appear unprofessional to some, but I believe the end justifies the means.

With a few exceptions, every column written appears in this book. I deleted those which proved to be incorrect in certain details or which were repetitious in content to other columns which appear in this book. The patterns are arranged in alphabetical order. Miscellaneous columns pertaining to an assortment of patterns, or those about lamps, novelties, cut glass, etc. appear at the back. Appropriate updated information pertaining to earlier columns has been added with an asterisk (*).

I owe so many people credit for helping me with my research these past several years, but I would like to take this opportunity to thank the publishers and editorial staff of the *Antique Trader* and *Glass Review* for their continued support. They gave me the exposure needed to "spread the word", which would not have been possible through my books alone. They also helped pay the bills when the books weren't selling. I also owe them my gratitude for allowing these reprints in book form, making the documentation within these covers available to new collectors, libraries and non-subscribers.

"APPLE & GRAPE IN SCROLL"
An Educated Guess Becomes Proven Fact!!

Last year, when I published the third volume of my series on pattern glass, illustrated among its pages was an emerald green cruet in a pattern which I called "Apple & Grape in Scroll." I got this name from collectors from whom I borrowed the cruet—and they could not recall from which source they acquired the name. I checked thoroughly, and to the best of my knowledge, that cruet was the first listed example of the pattern in modern glass literature.

Inasmuch as it was my first confrontation with the pattern, the information offered in my Book 3 was somewhat sketchy. I estimated the date of production at about 1905. I was unable to list any other examples made in the pattern, and in fact was skeptical that there even were any. However, shortly after publication of that volume, a reader wrote me informing me she had an emerald green toothpick holder in the same pattern, and I listed this item in the succeeding Book 4.

I have learned that attribution based upon pattern design or color characteristics can sometimes prove faulty. Book 3 states that *Apple & Grape in Scroll* was "probably" made by the Fostoria Glass Company of Moundsville, W. Va. I based this claim on the fact that the original stopper found in the illustrated cruet was the same one used in Fostoria's "Brazilian" pattern. Also, the two cruets were distinctly "teepee" shaped.

I am pleased to report now that this educated guess can be confirmed as a proven fact. Illustrated here are two catalog reprints from a rare original 1898 Fostoria Glass Company catalog. It was originally the Number 604 line, called "Cameo Ware." I believe that in order to avoid confusion with the "Cameo" pattern (ref. Lee) and the Cameo art glass, the *Apple & Grape in Scroll* name should be retained for future use.

This catalog proves particularly interesting since it illustrates several items in *A & G in S* not seen by this author. Also, it features the pattern in "opal" or Milk Glass. To date I have only witnessed it in emerald green with gold. The pages reprinted here are actually in color in the catalog, hand painted to show the customer how vividly decorated these pieces were.

Undoubtedly, this pattern underwent limited production as it is seldom seen today, and it remained unlisted by earlier glass writers. This is only one example of scores and scores of patterns which had escaped the attention of Kamm, Lee and Metz, proving that their great pioneer research in glass documentation must be continued.

No other pieces of *A & G in S* are shown in the catalog, and colors other than milk glass are not mentioned. It is possible that a few items were pressed in clear crystal, perhaps with gold decoration. The pattern is quite light in weight, of the mold blown variety, with the handles on the syrup, cream and water pitchers being applied.

It is interesting to note here that this catalog also illustrates Fostoria's popular *Atlanta* (better known today as "Late Lion") and *Carmen* patterns, both of which also had limited production in the same "Opal" colored glass.

FIGURE A—Reprint from rare 1898 Fostoria Glass Company catalogue, illustrating their No. 604 Cameo Ware, better known today as "Apple & Grape in Scroll"; note the original stopper to the cruet, upon which earlier undocumented attribution was based.

FIGURE B—Illustrations of the table and berry set, as well as a "breakfast size" creamer and covered sugar.

APPLE BLOSSOM—A STARTLING NORTHWOOD REDISCOVERY

As reported in this column two weeks ago, this week's featured pattern is frequently confused for the popular "Cosmos" line. Figure B illustrates a cruet in the "Apple Blossom" pattern, and indeed there are many similarities to Cosmos. Both have a netted background, both have raised, similarly designed, flowers and both are primarily found in hand-decorated opaque white milk glass. It is bewildering to me how the relatively common Cosmos line, with unknown (until now) origins, has risen to such substantial collectibility and value, whereas, the much rarer and equally lovely "Apple Blossom" line is frequently found begging at reasonable prices. Perhaps this somewhat startling announcement that our featured pattern is a Northwood creation will send a few of his devotees scurrying to acquire a few available pieces.

Illustrated in Figure A is a reprint of an ad which appeared in an 1896 issue of "China, Glass & Lamps." It proves almost nothing, except that the advertised line is decorated Opal (milk glass) ware. However, that same year, this interesting note appeared in a glass journal column, virtually substantiating my claim:

"The factory of the Northwood Co., Indiana, (Pa.), is putting one of the handsomest fine blown tableware sets on the market at present that we have seen for many a day. Made in fine lead opal, graceful as artistic blown goods only can be, with an apple blossom in relief, hand painted and tinted, this line is sure to prove a leader."

Kamm Volume 2, page 79, illustrates an "Apple Blossom" pattern which she names. The drawing appears to show an entirely different milk glass pattern. The description in her text reveals several uncanny similarities. Still, they are two distinctly different patterns—as Kamm's "Apple Blossom" has no netted background, and the foliage is not in relief. To avoid confusion, our featured pattern should heretofore be referred to as "Northwood's Apple Blossom."

There are other pattern characteristics which help substantiate this controversial Northwood attribution. Note the ribbed swirl effect of the pattern on the illustrated cruet. This same shape—in fact the shape on all pieces of "Northwood's Apple Blossom"—are identical to those on the corresponding pieces of Northwood's "Royal Ivy." This includes the shape of the salt shakers and even the miniature "night lamp."

Last month this column offered a Northwood heritage on at least a portion of the opalescent "Daisy & Fern" line. Notation was made that the molds for this week's featured pattern were also used in a variant of "Daisy & Fern" in colors of white, blue and cranberry opalescent.

These pieces should be referred to as "Daisy & Fern in Apple Blossom Mold" to distinguish them from the other variants. While "Daisy & Fern" has been massively reproduced, no reproductions have been made in the Apple Blossom molds.

I have often heard the ridiculous statement that "Northwood didn't make milk glass," this misconception couldn't be further from the truth. He was a brilliant color experimentalist and was responsible for many more patterns and colors than existing reference books give him credit for.

Apple Blossom

is the new line of decorated Opal tableware of

THE NORTHWOOD CO.

INDIANA, PA.

Blown Lemonade Sets, Novelties and Specialties in Flint, Opal and Color Combinations.

New line of lamps now ready.

WRITE FOR LITHOGRAPHS.

West, Carl Northwood.   New York, Alex. Menzies, 46 W. Broadway.

FIGURE A—1896 Northwood ad.

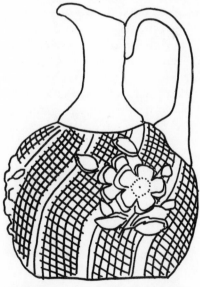

FIGURE B—"Apple Blossom" cruet

"BEAD AND DRAPE"

Illustrated is a reprint from a 1902 issue of "Glass and Pottery World" which I noticed while researching for a book. The lamp is in the pattern which is commonly referred to as "Bead and Drape" or "Beaded Drape" (the latter already designated for a different pattern). I had frequently heard this pattern referred to as Mt. Washington glass, but this ad, and others which I was fortunate to find, identify it as a pattern of the Pittsburgh Lamp, Brass & Glass Co., of Pittsburgh, Pa.

Not only made in lamps of several sizes (including a popular and much-reproduced miniature size), "Bead and Drape" was also produced in two sizes of cracker jars, a large round salad bowl, a bride's basket with frame, a celery vase, a jam jar, a water carafe and a four-piece table set (creamer, sugar, butter and spooner).* All but the basket have an applied metal rim, which carries over the beaded design found in the glass. The butter lid has a metal finial and a solid metal base, signed "M.S. Benedict Mfg. Co., Quadruple Plate."

Colors made include satin shades of "pigeon blood" red (originally advertised as "Cardinal"), pale turquoise blue (called "Azure"), lime green, and satin crystal. The beaded portion of the pattern usually lacks the satin finish, giving them a contrasting jewel-like appearance.

The man responsible for these exciting colors was the brilliant and little-known Nicholas Kopp, Jr., who earlier shared his skills with other glass companies (Hobbs, Brockunier and Consolidated Lamp & Glass). His contributions from circa 1889 to the end of the Victorian era were comparable even to those of the unsurpassable Mr. Northwood. Kopp was a designer (**Florette, Guttate,** even **Cosmos**) and an experimentalist in color who deserves considerable more recognition than he has received to date. My series on early colored glass will remedy his grave oversight.

"Bead and Drape" was revived for a time during the electricity era, as globes and shades can be found obviously designed for electrical fixtures. These have a solid satin finish and are not as smooth to the touch as the old. The miniature lamp has been reproduced for some time now and is today being made by L. G. Wright Glass Co., in colors of red, amber and white opaque satin, as well as shiny white opaque and a deep cranberry crystal (almost ruby red).

*Also known in syrup pitcher (squatty) and pickle caster.

10

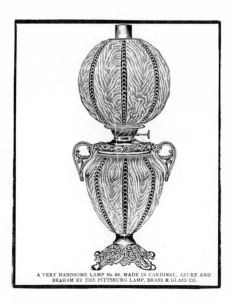

Fig. A—1902 ad featuring Bead and Rib lamp.

"BEATTY SWIRL"

This month I am featuring a popular opalescent pattern known as "Beatty Swirled Opal." Many collectors prefer to call it simply "Beatty Swirl." It was made around 1890 by A. J. Beatty & Sons of Steubenville, Ohio and continued after this company moved to Tiffin, Ohio and was absorbed into the giant U.S. Glass Company merger of 1891.

"Beatty Swirl" is illustrated here in a covered sugar bowl and a covered butter dish with the rare domed lid. The butter dish is most often found today with a flatter, only slightly domed cover. I have seen literally dozens of these butter dishes with flat lids, whereas the example shown here is the only one I have seen to date with a domed cover. However, I have been told of others by readers of my opalescent glass book (which illustrates the flat lid) so apparently two different molds were made for covering this butter dish.

"Beatty Swirl" is a pressed glass pattern, not to be confused with several "Swirl" patterns in mold-blown glass. It can be found in a four-piece table set (butter, creamer, sugar and spooner), a water set, a berry set (two shapes), a celery vase, a mug, a large round water tray, and a scarce syrup pitcher. Oddly enough, no toothpick holder, salt shaker or cruet is known to exist in the pattern.

The set was made primarily in opalescent white and blue. The tray to the water set has been often seen in yellow opalescent, which would lead one to expect other pieces in this color. However, none have been documented to date.

For beginning collectors who remain wary of reproduction pitfalls,

"Beatty Swirl" represents a wise choice for those susceptible to its simple charms. It has never been reproduced.

Beatty Swirl covered sugar and butter dish.

"BELLADONNA"

One of the sheer delights of glass research is turning up a pattern which has heretofore remained unlisted. It reminds us of how little we actually know, and brings anticipation of many future discoveries.

This week's featured pattern is listed here for the first time ever as far as I can ascertain. The pattern (Figure A) consists of a simple row of tiny beads at the base, paralleled by an attached row of tiny notches. The majority of the glass has no pattern in it at all, obviously designed to accommodate the delicate enamel decoration commonly found on this pattern. The butter dish lacks the beaded design.

Following the practice of earlier glass researchers, I have named this pattern *Belladonna*. I could have called it something sterile like "Beaded Base," but I felt that too many lovely patterns have already been undermined with unattractive pattern names.

It wasn't the least bit difficult learning which factory was responsible for production of *Belladonna,* as every piece seen to date has been signed with the familiar *N-in-a-Circle* trademark of H. Northwood & Company, of Wheeling, W. Va. The approximate date of manufacture would be around 1908.

One of the most startling features of this pattern is the colors it can be found in. Most often seen is the emerald green shade. Less frequently found is a deep sapphire blue color, not used on any of Northwood's earlier wares. Finally, and undoubtedly the most unnerving, is the rarely seen ruby-stained version of this pattern. I had previously thought, and reported in my Book I, that Northwood never *ever* produced ruby-stained glassware. Perhaps I was wrong in this assumption, but the likelihood is strong that an independent decorating firm bought large quantities of Northwood's crystal direct from the factory, and stained the glass on their own. I recently purchased a couple of pieces of Northwood's "Nearcut" pattern in ruby-stained glass, so I stand corrected at least in the claim that you will never find any of Northwood's wares in the popular ruby decorated glassware.

Belladonna was made only in the 4-piece table setting (butter, sugar, spooner and creamer), a water set and a berry set. Possibly a salt shaker was made, but it is unlikely. No other items have turned up to date.

Harry Northwood was involved in glass production in the United States for over 40 years, and only a fraction of his patterns have been deservingly credited to this brilliant glass craftsman. What a shame that we may never know just how massive his contributions really were!

Fig. A. "Belladonna" spooner and covered butter.

"BLOCKED THUMBPRINT BAND"

This month I am featuring a pattern which I named BLOCKED THUMBPRINT when I wrote my first book in 1974. Shortly after publication, I noticed Kamm used this name for another pattern, so I revised the name in the second edition to BLOCKED THUMBPRINT BAND, to prevent confusion with the Kamm pattern.

When I wrote the first book (using toothpick holders to illustrate patterns), I speculated that the pattern was made by the U.S. Glass Company. This was based primarily upon my instincts, which this time proved incorrect. I now know that BLOCKED THUMBPRINT BAND was a product of the Duncan & Miller Glass Company of Washington, Pennsylvania. It was made in a complete table service, primarily in crystal, but also in limited ruby-stained crystal. The pattern dates about 1902.

The photograph shown here was taken at the Carl Johnson Antique Show in Dallas, Texas, illustrating a water set in our featured pattern. Other than the fact that this is the first water set I have seen in this pattern, it is even more unique because of the unusual pebbly decoration with which it is graced. Each tumbler has a different scene of what appears to be Nursery Rhyme animals and birds, including a cat, rabbits, geese, ducks, deer, chicks, etc. The pitcher itself is adorned with an angelic figure, which perhaps is meant to be Mother Nature, or some mythological figure depicting a goddess protector of animals.

The name "Martha" is written in script on each tumbler. It is unusual even more so to note that this decoration must have been applied at the Duncan factory, because the handle to the pitcher covers a portion of the angel wings.

The decoration on this set is similar to the pebbled finish found on patterns like REVERSE SWIRL, CHRYSANTHEMUM BASE and PANELLED SPRIG. This is my first experience witnessing this finish being used as figural decoration, and in all honesty, it isn't very pretty. Perhaps it was awkward to work with, and the results not satisfactory.

Credit for discovering who made BLOCKED THUMBPRINT BAND must be shared with my co-author on Book 5, Fred Bickenheuser, who has several rare catalogs in his files. He most unselfishly allowed me to study them for proper documentation, and I want to express my appreciation once again.

Previously unattributed ruby-stained water set in BLOCKED THUMBPRINT BAND, made by Duncan & Miller Glass Company, circa 1902.

"BLOOMS AND BLOSSOMS"
ANOTHER NORTHWOOD "SLEEPER"

A "sleeper," in collector's jargon, is an item which is acquired by a lucky or knowledgeable individual from another individual who has little or no knowledge of value or rarity. In simpler words, a "sleeper" is a rare or valuable item which rests unappreciated with one owner until someone who is aware of its value comes along and wakes it up.

This week I will be "waking up" a few collectors who follow this column by presenting information on a Northwood pattern called *"Blooms & Blossoms"* which until now was known only in the salt shaker shown by Peterson (he called it "Flower & Bud") and the blue opalescent handled olive dish shown in the second volume of my series.

Illustrated here for the first time is a tumbler in this same pattern, which virtually assures the existence of a water pitcher. The tumbler is in clear glass with color-stained flowers, blooms and leaves. This hand-decoration is in lovely "rainbow" effect, as each petal of the flower is painted a different color, with the stippled background remaining clear. The threading is also colorstained.

This tumbler is not marked with any trademark. However, I have personally seen a small berry dish in this pattern in marigold carnival glass which had the familiar "N-in-a-Circle" trademark of Harry Northwood & Company of Wheeling, W. Va. This carnival dish also confirms the existence of the pattern in marigold, and that a berry set was also made. Late Note: Just noticed where Rose Presznick does list a plate in this pattern. She calls it "Lightning Flower."

The Northwood trademark dates production of *Blooms & Blossoms* after 1906, when use of this signature first began. It is quite possible that the pattern had extremely limited production in emerald green with gold, and perhaps a piece other than the olive dish can be found in opalescent white, blue or green. However, any piece of *Blooms & Blossoms* should be considered scarce, since I have personally been searching for an item to photograph for three years (other than the inconsequential novelties), and this tumbler proves to be a very important find.

It can now be confirmed a four-piece table set was made, since I have seen one. The water set and berry set are also confirmed. A rare cruet is also known.

Northwood Blooms & Blossoms tumbler and rare salt shaker.

THE "BLOWN DRAPE" PATTERN

This week I am featuring updated information on a pattern in blown opalescent glass which Hartung named *Blown Drape.* The pitcher and tumbler are illustrated here. This pattern was listed in Book 2 of my series, but no illustration and little data was available at the time of that 1975 publication.

This limited data was the direct result of so little attention being directed toward *blown opalescent pattern glass* by earlier researchers. The probable reason for this is that this glass was not very popular until recently. Earlier glass research was concentrated in more popular fields, such as pressed glass (Kamm, Lee), art glass (Revi, Grover), carnival glass (Hartung, Presznick), custard glass (Gaddis, Bramer) and Sandwich glass (Lee, McKearin). Prior to 1975, confusion was rampant in this field. The same patterns were known by different names, many were never named at all, and most collectors were avoiding investing in glass which they believed was widely reproduced. With such a void in documentation, new collectors feared to tread on unfamiliar ground.

How things have changed in the past three years!! Now blown opalescent glass is equally as popular as the pressed glass variety, and new research information is turning up around every corner. The value of many patterns has practically doubled as new collectors join the ranks every week, decreasing the supply at the same time they increase the demand.

The *Blown Drape* pattern shown here in cranberry was also made in opalescent white, blue and green. Care should be taken not to confuse this with the very similar *Blown Twist,* which has the same pattern, but has been twisted at a sharp angle causing the "drapes" to lean sharply to the right.

There is another mold-blown drapery type pattern which I incorrectly attributed to Jefferson Glass in my Book 2. This pattern should hereafter be referred to as "Fenton Drape," as it appeared in their 1910 catalog. The unique feature about this Fenton pattern, known only in a water set, is that the pitcher is mold-blown and the tumbler is pressed. Unlike the *Blown Drape* pitcher shown here, which is tankard shaped, the *Fenton Drape* pattern is much shorter, bulbous in shape, with a ruffled top. The Fenton variant can be found only in white, blue and green opalescent, with no known cranberry version. I have also seen the mold used on a decorated marigold carnival water pitcher, which is very rare, and to the best of my knowledge, previously unlisted. Decorated ruby is also known.

Blown Drape was listed as "possibly Northwood" in my Book 2. Hartung dated it from an early ad in her files which dates its production between 1900 and 1905. My speculative Northwood attribution can now be somewhat confirmed with the discovery of several shards in this pattern which were unearthed at Northwood's Indiana, Pennsylvania factory dump site. The ad dates coincide with Northwood's personal departure from this factory, in 1902, to set up his Wheeling, West Virginia plant. Much has been written by this author concerning the "Northwood-Dugan" association at Indiana, Pa., and I will not be repetitious here. I will state again, however, it makes little difference whether certain patterns made at Indiana, Pennsylvania during the transitional period (1900 to 1905) are Northwood or Dugan. Both firms produced glass with comparable quality control, and many patterns were made originally by Northwood and continued by Dugan for several years thereafter. Trying to ascertain who made what and when can often prove a researcher's nightmare.

Blown Drape was made only in the water set and in a barber bottle. No table set, berry set, cruet, syrup pitcher, toothpick holder or sugar shaker have ever been documented in this pattern. However, since the similar Blown Twist was made in a sugar shaker, it is possible that a rare sugar shaker exists in Blown Drape.

Rare cranberry opalescent BLOWN DRAPE water pitcher and tumbler, made by Northwood, circa 1903.

"BOHEMIAN GRAPE"
Another Unlisted Pattern

This week I am featuring a truly beautiful colored glass patern which to date remained unlisted in existing literature on pattern glass. I am naming this pattern "Bohemian Grape" in my Book 5 which is soon to be published.

At first glance this appears to be the "Bohemian" pattern, a popular line produced by the U.S. Glass Company around 1900. "Bohemian" was previously featured in this column, and you will recall that it is sometimes popularly referred to as "Floradora." Ironically, this other pattern is frequently confused for the similar "Delaware" pattern.

The obvious similarities between "Bohemian" and *Bohemian Grape* are the unique scroll design at the top and bottom of the pattern, as well as the wave-like stippling in the background. However, *Bohemian Grape* does not have the distinct flower found on "Bohemian" and it is not a footed pattern. All items except the tumbler and covered butter are footed in the "Bohemian" pattern.

It is my belief that both patterns were produced by U.S. Glass, the huge conglomerate of 17 different companies which merged in 1891. I am not only basing this claim on the obvious pattern design similarities, but also on the colors of green with gold and a deep "rose" with gold in which I have seen *Bohemian Grape*. These colors are identical to those in which both "Delaware" and "Bohemian" were made.

One unique feature about *Bohemian Grape* is that it is made in only one "set." Illustrated here is the tankard pitcher and tumblers to what I believe is a breakfast "juice set." The tumblers are not quite 3½ inches tall, less than ¾ the size of a standard water tumbler. The tankard is only 10½ inches tall, and both items are so tall and lean in shape that they would be virtually useless as a lemonade or water set. The tumblers would hardly be able to accommodate the chunk ice used at the turn of the century. I am fairly certain that this set was used for orange or grape juice at the breakfast table.

Bohemian Grape was made in no other items and dates around 1900. It is extremely hard to find today and undoubtedly underwent a considerably limited production. Other possible colors are crystal with gold and frosted crystal, but I have seen neither of these colors to date.

Scarce "Bohemian Grape" breakfast set tankard and juice tumblers in a rich emerald green with gold. Note the applied handle on this mold-blown pattern.

BROKEN COLUMN

BROKEN COLUMN is a very popular pattern made from as early as 1887 to as late as 1900. It was produced primarily in crystal, sometimes with the notches stained red, but a few limited items have been reported in cobalt blue. BROKEN COLUMN was originally made by the Columbia Glass Company at Findlay, Ohio. It was so popular that production was continued after this factory was acquired by the giant merger, the United States Glass Company.

For years, I was told of the existence of a toothpick holder in BROKEN COLUMN, but I never had the opportunity to examine one personally. It is most definitely a very rare little item. When it was described to me, the perfectly flat top made me wary of the possibility it could be a salt shaker of which the top was ground. Yet I always was open-minded enough not to completely rule out the possibility of the existence of such a rarity.

In my Book 3, I stated "toothpick not yet documented." In my book *1,000 Toothpick Holders,* I listed the BROKEN COLUMN toothpick holder as undocumented. I was beginning to give up all hope of ever proving this piece existed.

Well, here it is folks! I wish it were a photograph, but instead I am offering here an almost perfect line drawing (near actual size) of the

BROKEN COLUMN toothpick holder. It is just under 2¼ inches tall, with a perfect 1" diameter hole in the center. The top is perfectly flat, just like a chopped off salt shaker, but the toothpick holder is much larger in circumference. Also you will notice how close the second row of notches is to the top row of half notches. On the salt shaker the notches (rows) are more equally spaced.

Yet, I must warn you about the possibility of investing in a ground down salt shaker. The value of toothpick holders is rising faster than my price guides can be revised, so beware of so called toothpick holders with perfectly flat tops.

BROKEN COLUMN remains a relatively safe investment. Only the goblet has been reproduced to date, in crystal only. In ruby stained crystal, it's true of the toothpick holder. In ruby stain, I believe a BROKEN COLUMN toothpick holder would be worth at least $250.

I would like to express my deepest appreciation to June Paxton for sending this toothpick holder to me for examination and verification. I am very grateful to her and dozens of others like her who have taken the time and energy to share their discoveries with the rest of us.

LATE NOTE: At the time I wrote the above I was unaware of the reproductions being sponsored by the Smithsonian Institution. I can only assume they have had them marked as reproductions. Included among several items are a creamer and covered sugar (the lid has no finial) which sells for $24 retail per set. Only clear is offered with NO TOOTHPICK holder among the reproduced items.

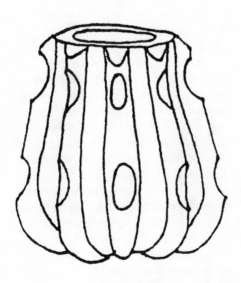

"BULGING LOOPS"
Another Testament to the Kopp Genius

It doesn't take much study and research to ascertain who was responsible for the design and creation of this week's featured pattern. It was obviously a product of the Consolidated Lamp & Glass Company, circa 1895. The shapes and colors of the illustrated items are virtually identical to other known Consolidated patterns, such as "Florette," "Guttate," and "Cone." These other patterns have reached a substantial degree of popularity among collectors of fine Victorian colored glass, and yet "Bulging Loops" has remained out of the limelight for quite some time now. Perhaps this is due to the fact that, to date, it has remained unattributed in the many volumes available on pattern identification. Or perhaps it is due to its simplicity of design, compared to the more ornate trio listed above.

Despite this, "Bulging Loops" was created in such excitingly beautiful colors, that it is consistently bought up when it appears on the market. It is frequently found at such reasonable prices (unlisted patterns usually are) that the buyers cannot resist the tempting colors. "Bulging Loops" is the only pattern made to a considerable degree in a bright yellow cased glass. True lemon yellow opaque glass is very rare in Victorian ware, and this pattern was made in a complete set in this color.

Our featured pattern is also available in a complete set of pigeon blood red, and has become very collectible in this color. This true deep red crystal is also scarce, and "Bulging Loops" is available in a complete table service in this exciting color. Many collectors have purchased pieces of this pigeon blood colored pattern, not even aware that it is a form of pattern glass. The cracker jar and water pitcher are most often seen, but I have owned several other shapes—listed at the end of this column.

"Bulging Loops" is also available in beautiful satin finish colors of yellow, pink and blue. This blue shade defies description. You have to see it to believe it! It is created differently from the other opaque colors, consisting of an outer layer of deep blue crystal and in inner lining of white. The combination of these two castings is definitely a color technique solely used by Nicholas Kopp, Jr., who headed the production of Consolidated (and two other companies) and who was a color genius comparable even to the "incomparable" Harry Northwood. Both men came from European families with long backgrounds in glassmaking, and their contributions to the production of Victorian colored glassware are endless.

"Bulging Loops" also comes in plain opaque colors, without casings of crystal on the outside or a white lining on the inside, and these colors are not as popular today.

Nicholas Kopp was a color experimentalist, and certain rare pieces of this pattern can be found in cranberry (with or without an inner casing of white), and red satin. This latter color is very popular today. It is actually the pigeon blood color with an acidized satin finish. Most of the red satin lamps found today (except for the reproductions, naturally), were designed or indirectly created through the efforts of the long-overlooked color genius, Nicholas Kopp, Jr.

Our featured pattern is available in many, many shapes. Some are seen frequently, others are very, very rare. These include a complete water set, table set (creamer, sugar, butter, spooner), berry set, salt & pepper, mustard, celery vase, syrup jug, sugar shaker, cruet, toothpick holder, and cracker jar. The cracker jar usually has a metal rim, lid and bail—although it is possible that a glass lid was also made.

A final note of thanks here to Mel Murray (author of "History of Fostoria, Ohio Glass") for substantiating my theory regarding this pattern. I wrote him before publishing my findings in my book, and he answered confirming that some glass shards were recently dug up at Consolidated's Fostoria plant.

A group of "Bulging Loops" pieces.

23

"BULLSEYE & BUTTON"

This month I am featuring a pattern about which very little has been written to date. It is called "Bullseye and Button," a name given to it by Murray in his cruet book. When I wrote my Book 3, only the cruet, syrup pitcher and toothpick holder could be documented in the pattern. Since then, I now know of the table set (illustrated) and water set. Undoubtedly a berry set was also made.

Before I saw this table set, all the items I saw in "Bullseye and Button" were in crystal and emerald green, without gold decoration. The set illustrated here has a rich gilding applied to the finials, rims and on the button portion of the pattern.

Who actually made this lovely pattern is still not known, but it dates around 1895 to 1900. It undoubtedly underwent limited production, as it is very rarely seen on today's collector market. I hate to speculate about manufacturers, but this pattern is very characteristic of the Riverside Glass Company—especially in the rich emerald green.

The pattern has never been reproduced and represents a safe investment to glass lovers wary of reproductions.

THE "CADMUS" PATTERN
It's later than you think.

This week I am featuring a pattern which was named CADMUS by Millard in his goblet book. He reported the pattern was made in the 1880s in clear only. Both Metz and the Unitt's show goblets in *Cadmus,* and agree with Millard's dating of the pattern.

However, reprinted here is an original ad from a December, 1902, issue of the "Crockery and Glass Journal", which clearly illustrates our featured pattern. It was made by the Beaumont Glass Company at their Grafton, West Virginia location. Beaumont, who was Harry Northwood's brother-in-law, had a factory previously at Martins Ferry, Ohio.

The ad shown here clearly states that the page shows "a few pieces of our 1903 line of tableware." This seems to imply that additional items were also made in the pattern, and that it was called their "No. 1903." This same statement could also be interpreted to mean that the pieces shown were just a few of their lines for the year 1903. But the key word is the singular use of the word "line"—not "lines."

The Unitt's report the pattern was made in clear and color, but I have never seen a piece of *Cadmus* in color to date. Also, I cannot be certain that any pieces were made other than those listed in the ad, although it seems likely a water pitcher was in the line. The Beaumont Glass Company didn't prosper very well at their new Grafton location, and probably newly molded patterns were being cut back to only a few essential shapes.

Cadmus is not often seen today, and it even failed to be listed by the great pattern glass pioneers, Kamm and Lee. Perhaps it wasn't as good a seller as its makers hoped it would be.

*A toothpick holder is also known in this pattern.

"THE CATHEDRAL PATTERN"

Illustrated this month is a rather unusual reprint from an 1891 catalog of the United States Glass Company, Factory B (Bryce Brothers, Pittsburgh). The condition of the original was very poor, with scotch tape and big red marks across the page, but the information on this page made it worthy of inclusion in my Book 5.

The name of the pattern I am featuring is *Cathedral,* a name used by collectors for years before the original name "Orion" was discovered. Both Kamm and Lee endorsed the collectors' name for the pattern. However, there is one interesting feature about this design which somehow makes the name *Cathedral* inappropriate. Not all pieces of the pattern have the church window-like design. Note the unusual covered butter, never properly documented, which for years has probably been sold as anything but *Cathedral.*

It was obvious Kamm was not aware of this particular facet when she listed the individual cream pitcher in her Book 2 as "Waffle and Fine Cut," a name by which the butter dish has probably been sold. The cruet, shown here with original stopper, also has the W&FC motif, as opposed to the characteristics of *Cathedral.* However, all of these pieces belong to the same set and should hereafter be referred to by one name.

The pattern was first made in the mid-1880s and probably continued after the U.S. Glass merger for several years. *Cathedral* is known in crystal, amber, pale blue, vaseline, limited amethyst and apple green, and ruby-stained crystal. No toothpick holder or salt shaker is known.

Cathedral has never been reproduced and represents a safe investment for collectors today.

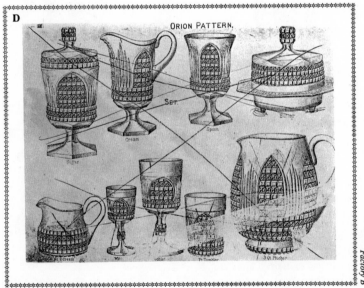

PLATE A—Page from 1891 U.S. Glass Co. catalog, illustrating Cathedral (Orion) pattern.

Plate B—Cathedral pattern cruet in amber, previously known as "Waffle & Fine Cut."

Plates in this pattern have been reported in a depression "pink", obviously a late reissue.

"CHRISTMAS SNOWFLAKE"

The pattern I named CHRISTMAS SNOWFLAKE in my second book has become extremely popular in the past years, but its origins are still surrounded with mystery. When I wrote that book I was unaware of the variant of the pattern without the ribbed mold, which seems to lend credence to the theory that the pattern was made by two different companies. I presented this information in one of my columns two years ago, but additional information has turned up which should be presented here.

Illustrated here is a blue opalescent CHRISTMAS SNOWFLAKE water pitcher at the left and a ribbed version of the pattern in cranberry on the right. The pitcher on the right has been attributed by local Wheeling area residents to Hobbs, Brockunier and Company around 1885-1890. Even with the approval of the local Oglebay Museum, this remains nothing more than a possibility. We have no catalogues or ads on which to base this attribution.

However, a Northwood letterhead from around 1897 illustrates an artist's rendition of a grouping of Northwood products, among them being a vase with definite characteristics of CHRISTMAS SNOWFLAKE. To date this is the only appearance of the pattern in any kind of early documentation, so we can at least confirm the fact that Northwood had something to do with this pattern. The really odd fact is that I never even heard of a "vase" in this pattern, only the water sets.

CHRISTMAS SNOWFLAKE is made in white, blue and cranberry opalescent. The ribbed variant was recently reported in blue, quite rare. Prices quoted below are for items in mint condition.*

CHRISTMAS SNOWFLAKE

Item:	White Opales.	Blue Opales.	Cranberry Opales.
water pitcher, plain	$ 75	$250	$350
water pitcher, ribbed	100	295	350
tumbler, plain	20	40	50
tumbler, ribbed	22	45	55
vase (undocumented)	30	65	85
cruet (rare)	150	300	350

*Reproductions have recently appeared on the market, in cranberry and cobalt blue opalescent. New items include a cruet, pitcher and tumbler, pickle caster insert, milk pitcher. The only old cruet seen was in Northwood's "Parian Swirl" mold.

"NORTHWOOD COINSPOT"

If there is one single blown opalescent pattern responsible for more confusion than any other it would have to be COINSPOT. To start with, it is known by many different names, among them Coin Dot, Polka Dot, Dot, Thumbprint—but COINSPOT is the single name I endorsed in my book on opalescent glass. In addition to the name confusion, we are dealing here with a pattern which was made by at least eight different companies over a period of forty years—and that doesn't consider Fenton's production of the pattern in the late 1920s and the L. G. Wright reproductions from the last twenty years. Needless to say, the "over-production" of COINSPOT has limited the popularity of this pattern on the collectible glass market, not to mention the fact that the pattern is too simple for most collectors' tastes.

The secret to collecting this pattern successfully is to know which shapes are good and which are not. I listed eight different variations of COINSPOT in my Book 2, but now I know of more. Two of these are illustrated here, both made by Northwood after 1905. Both of the water pitchers shown are in blue opalescent, and both are signed with the distinctive "N-in-a-Circle" trademark of H. Northwood and Company, Wheeling, W.Va.

It is unusual to find the Northwood trademark on a piece of mold-blown glassware, but the examples shown here are not singular rarities. I have also seen a pink-cased bride's bowl, and a decorated cranberry pickle castor insert, both with the "N-in-a-Circle." Usually this popular trademark is found on Northwood's *pressed* glass after 1904.

This pitcher and tumbler shown in Figure A are both mold blown; both signed. I have only seen this set in white and blue opalescent. Cranberry opalescent would be a choice find. The pitcher is also known in non-opalescent crystal, with the trademark. When the "dots" are not white, the pattern is popularly known as "Inverted Thumbprint," *another* mold-blown pattern made by almost a dozen different companies.

Figure B illustrates another pitcher, signed Northwood, which I have seen with five tumblers, all sitting on a pressed glass, round-shaped, blue opalescent tray. I am not absolutely positive, but I recall the tray was signed Northwood also. The set was priced at $350, so I left it sitting on the dealer's shelf.

Other companies responsible for the many variations of COINSPOT are listed below in chronological order. It is interesting to note that Northwood was very influential in the production at Hobbs, Brockunier & Co. when this firm first introduced COINSPOT.

HOBBS, BROCKUNIER & CO., Wheeling, W.Va. (1885-1892)
BELMONT GLASS COMPANY, Bellaire, O. (circa 1887)
BUCKEYE GLASS COMPANY, Martins Ferry, O. (circa 1889)
BEAUMONT GLASS CO., Martins Ferry, O. (circa 1900)
NORTHWOOD GLASS CO., Wheeling, W.Va. (1903-1908)
JEFFERSON GLASS CO., Steubenville, O. (after 1905)

DUGAN GLASS CO., Indiana, Pa. (1904-1912)
FENTON ART GLASS CO., Williamstown, W.Va. (circa 1912)

This list is only those with *known* production of COINSPOT. Each company had distinct shapes in their Coinspot designs. The only case where this is not true involves the acquisition by Beaumont Glass Company of molds from the disbanded Hobbs factory after 1892. Just a few of the "variants" in Coinspot are *Ribbed Coinspot, Nine-Panel Coinspot* and *Square-top Coinspot.*

Deciding which company made which variant is not always an easy undertaking. It is rare to find an early ad featuring mold-blown opalescent patterns, and determining the manufacturer often is a matter of conjecture. However, Mr. Northwood made my job a breeze when he decided to add his trademark to the two pitchers shown here and I will be forever indebted to him for his foresight.

FIGURE A—Blue opalescent ruffle-top Coinspot pitcher and tumbler by Northwood.

FIGURE B—Northwood Coinspot water pitcher with crimped top.

"COLUMNED THUMBPRINTS"

This month I am featuring a pattern which was named COLUMNED THUMBPRINTS in Kamm Book 5, page 71. This toothpick isn't exactly unlisted (it appears in Mighell's book on the subject), but I am showing it here for better pattern detail and to reveal newly found information.

This line was made only in crystal, with the toothpick shown in an early Sears catalogue which featured a grouping of COLUMNED THUMBPRINTS. It was referred to, oddly enough, as the "West Moreland Assortment." This seems to imply that the Westmoreland Glass Company could have made the pattern, since I doubt that Sears pulled that name out of a hat for no reason.

The toothpick is an extremely attractive one, with a unique combination of circles, slashes, diamonds and stars, totaling up to a very busy imitation cut pattern. In mint condition, this one should be worth about $30 and should be considered scarce.

(Reprinted courtesy National Toothpick Holder Collectors' Society)

"CONSOLIDATED'S CRISS-CROSS"

Many mold blown opalescent patterns verge so close on being considered art glass that their prices are frequently comparable. Among these elite lines is certainly "Royal Ivy," very popular in the frosted rubina and rainbow spatter. The same is true of the long unlisted "Leaf Mold", available in several semi-art glass variations.

It is simply astounding that literally dozens of blown opalescent patterns have been virtually ignored in books on pattern identification.

This week's featured pattern is another of those long-unlisted lines which unfortunately has lead many unsuspecting collectors and dealers to believe it is some form of rare art glass—probably due to a striking resemblance to characteristics of Findlay Rose Onyx.

Illustrated in Figure A is a line drawing of a toothpick holder and Figure B offers a close-up photograph of a salt shaker. The pattern is a series of X-like figures, one on top of another. These little crosses are slightly raised out, which may be the reason for the Onyx-like look and feel—especially apparent in the satin finish. On smaller pieces, the little crosses are short and fat, on larger pieces these Xs are more spread out and become thinner lines.

It was in 1972 that the first information regarding this pattern surfaced. A considerable number of shards were dug up at the plant site of the Consolidated Lamp and Glass Company at Fostoria, Ohio, (established in 1894), with these findings being reported by Melvin Murray in his "History of Fostoria, Ohio Glass." I had the privilege of rummaging through these shards, and it was a constant delight to witness the dozens of colors (many experimental) which were created at the Consolidated factory around 1894. Mr. Murray calls the pattern "Criss-Cross" in his book, but perhaps the name "Consolidated's Criss-Cross" would be more proper to avoid confusion with other similarly designed opalescent patterns.

The home office of Consolidated Lamp & Glass was in Pittsburgh, Pa., but actual production took place at their Fostoria, Ohio factory in 1894-1895. After that year, production personnel moved to their new factory at Corapolis, Pa. However, due to the extreme scarcity of our featured pattern, I feel that its production was limited to the 1894 season.

Again, we find Nicholas Kopp, Jr. as the man behind the pattern. He headed production for Consolidated for several years. This pattern was produced only in cranberry, rubina and crystal opalescent glass, both shiny and frosted. "Consolidated's Criss-Cross" certainly attests to Mr. Kopp's versatility, as the company is noted more for its cased and satin opaque glass colors. But it must be recalled here that Mr. Kopp was previously associated with The Hobbs Glass Company, Wheeling, W.Va., who earlier (as Hobb's, Brockunier & Co.) was world famous for this type of blown opalescent ware, also in both shiny and satin finish. Were it not for Mr. Murray's diggings at the old Consolidated factory site, the "Criss-Cross" line would undoubtedly be considered a Hobbs' product by students of early pattern glass.

"Consolidated's Criss-Cross" was produced in a complete table service.

This includes the 4-piece table set, the water set, the berry set, a toothpick, cruet, sugar shaker, mustard, salt & pepper, finger bowl, syrup, and celery vase.

FIGURE A—"Consolidated Criss-Cross" toothpick holder.

FIGURE B—Salt Shaker (Photo by J.H. Kemp, Jr.)

FIGURE C—A pitcher in "Consolidated's Criss-Cross". Note how thin the lines are in the lattice.

THE "COREOPSIS" PATTERN

Illustrated here is a rare unlisted cruet in a pattern called COREOPSIS by Kamm in her book 5. In milk glass it is very similar in design and decoration to the popular Cosmos pattern. When I wrote my Book 3 of my pattern glass series in 1976, I speculated that it was a product of Nicholas Kopp while he was with the Consolidated Lamp & Glass Company of Coraopolis, Pennsylvania. I was also unaware of the existence of this cruet at that time.

Nicholas Kopp was a genius in the creation of opaque colored glass at the turn of the century. He began his brilliant career where other famous glassmakers got their starts (Northwood, Beaumont, etc.)—at the Hobbs Glass Company in Wheeling. At the age of 23 he assumed the position of manager of Consolidated Lamp and Glass Company at Fostoria, Ohio. The following year, in 1895, the factory burned down and the firm moved to Coraopolis.

In an 1896 issue of "China, Glass & Lamps", the following note appeared concerning a visit to the new factory at Coraopolis, "Mr. Nicholas Kopp, the manager, designer and metal maker, has developed a versatility and resourcefulness in designing decorations, shapes and fine metal shadings, which his most intimate friends never expected him possessed of."

The report went on to state, "The great variety of lamps and globes especially attracts the attention of the visitor at these works. President (J. B.) Graham reports that the Consolidated has thus far done the largest lamp business ever recorded, and far in excess of that done by any single manufacturing firm in the world."

Thus we can see that Kopp's genius in the field of opaque and cased colored glass was especially successful when used to its fullest potential as a source of lighting. An ad in February, 1896, extolled Consolidated's "Cerise", a color they claimed was never before successfully made in transparent glassware. The ad went on to state "The color is NOT RUBY, but a peculiarly rich coral-red; the red that is seen upon a half-ripe cherry." It is my belief that this ad refers to the color we now call "Pigeon Blood."

But by far, Kopp's most popular color was originally called "Roman Ruby"—which today we call red satin glass. This color was introduced in 1898, and an ad for that year claimed that this new color was being praised in two new lines of tableware. I have no absolute proof that our featured *Coreopsis* pattern was made by Consolidated, but it *is* made in red satin glass in a table set, water set and berry set. It can also be found in a squatty and tall syrup, a cracker jar, and the rare cruet.

The butter dish to the table set has a metal base, and sometimes, especially in the case of red satin, the other pieces to the set will have attached metal rims and handles. The cracker jar can have either a metal or a glass lid.

The opaque white or milk glass version of *Coreopsis* can be found in either shiny or satin finish. The red satin version has white painted decoration in a most pleasant effect.

It should be noted here that Kopp did not stay with Consolidated during his entire career. He shared his knowledge and expertise with the giant Pittsburgh Lamp, Brass and Glass Company after its formation in 1902. Here he called his red satin "Venetian Ruby", and a trade journal at that time referred to Kopp as, "the greatest glass chemist in the world", a statement with which I have little argument.

FIGURE A — Rare and previously unlisted cruet in COREOPSIS pattern.

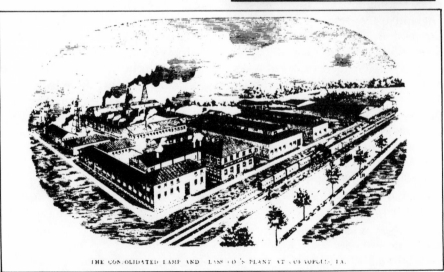

THE CONSOLIDATED LAMP AND GLASS CO.'S PLANT AT COROAPOLIS, PA.

FIGURE B — Aerial view of Consolidated Lamp and Glass Company's factory at Coraopolis, Pa.

"THE CORNFLOWER PATTERN"

In the past three years this column has devoted considerable attention to the unlisted patterns of Harry Northwood, perhaps the greatest single contributor to the colored table glass market at the turn-of-the-century. This week I will concentrate on one of Northwood's associates, Thomas E. A. Dugan, and a glass pattern produced at his Dugan Glass Company.

Illustrated here are four items in a pattern I have named *Cornflower*. The water pitcher and tumbler are in a deep emerald green with silver decoration on the flowers and swirling stalks. The decanter and wine glass are in the same shade of green, only with gold decoration on the pattern. The design on the two sets is similar, but not exactly alike. However, both sets have a distinctive oval-framed flower amidst those flowing stalks, so I feel it is perfectly acceptable to have these two sets carry the same pattern name.

Attributing this pattern to the Dugan Glass Company would have been mere speculation, were it not for the shards in *Cornflower* unearthed at the Indiana, Pennsylvania factory dump site. Illustrated next to the wine glass is a portion of the stem from a clear *Cornflower* wine. However, even without these indisputable shards, *Cornflower's* silver decoration is typically Dugan. Also, I have seen the water set in an ivory-colored custard glass (with silver decoration), which matched perfectly the custard color of the "Diamond Maple Leaf" and "Diamonds & Clubs" patterns.

Other colors, besides crystal, in which the pattern may be found are cobalt blue, and possibly a rare piece in carnival glass. No items other than the water and wine sets are known in *Cornflower*, although it is possible that it was made in a vase or novelty bowl of some kind.

The Thomas Dugan story is an interesting one, especially because of his close association with his nephew Harry Northwood. Mr. Dugan was born in England in 1865, came to America in 1881, where he soon worked for Hobbs, Brockunier at Wheeling, W.Va. He then worked in Pittsburgh for a time, when he was offered a position at the Buckeye Glass Company (Martins Ferry, O.), managed by Northwood himself. Then began a close business association which lasted for three decades. When Northwood relocated to Elwood City, Pennsylvania, Dugan went with him as his foreman. He retained this position when Northwood made his next move to Indiana, Pennsylvania.

When Northwood himself left this factory—after the ill-fated merger into the National Glass Company—Dugan stayed on as manager of the company. In 1904, the concern was sold and reorganized under the name of the Dugan Glass Company. This firm continued to manufacture many of the popular patterns introduced while Northwood still held the reigns.

All too often I have been quick to point out that, even though Northwood no longer physically managed the Indiana, Pa. factory after 1902, his influence remained throughout the long life of this company. Perhaps I was short-sighted in not recognizing the contributions of Thomas Dugan. The following quote appeared in "INDIANA COUNTY PENNSYL-

VANIA—HER PEOPLE, PAST AND PRESENT", published in 1913:

"The company has been successful from the start under the efficient management of Mr. Dugan, who is a recognized authority and expert in his line. The product of the plant is shipped to both coasts and there is also considerable export business. The magnitude of the output may be judged from the fact that employment is given to about 200 and 30 hands in all departments . . . Much of the success of the company is justly attributed to the complete knowledge Mr. Dugan has of the various phases of the business, for he is not only an excellent judge of workmanship and finished goods, but he also understands the marketing question and keeps abreast of progress in every department . . ."

This column on *Cornflower* and Thomas Dugan would not have been possible were it not for the unselfish contributions of Indiana, Pennsylvania resident Del Helman. Mr. Helman has an avid interest in the glassware made in his home town, and has mailed me thousands and thousands of glass shards which he and his family unearthed at the Northwood-Dugan factory dump site. He also sent me the information about Thomas Dugan, about whom very little was known until now. Perhaps someday Mr. Dugan can come out of the shadow of his famous nephew Harry Northwood, and receive full acknowledgement for his singular contributions to the table glass field. My deepest appreciation is extended here to Mr. Helman for his part in making this a possibility.

FIGURE A—Rare CORNFLOWER water pitcher and tumbler, emerald green with silver decoration.

FIGURE B—CORNFLOWER wine glass and decanter (stopper is not original) in emerald green with gold decoration. The piece of glass on the left is one of several shards used to attribute this pattern.

"COSMOS"

Perhaps the most collectible and expensive pattern in milk glass is "Cosmos". And yet to date its maker (or makers) has not been identified in the many volumes available on pattern identification. This week I will report my findings regarding this extremely popular line, and offer other important data regarding similar milk glass patterns frequently confused for "Cosmos."

According to Kamm book 5, pg. 53, this pattern had been popularly known as "Cosmos" for many years, despite the fact that the pattern's floral design contains not a single one. The original manufacturer's name was, more appropriately, "Daisy."

Illustrated in Figure A is a 1902 ad reprint which identifies The Consolidated Lamp and Glass Co., of Coraopolis, Pa., as at least partly responsible for production of "Cosmos." It was also earlier made, circa 1894, at this same company's Fostoria, Ohio plant. Recent diggings at the factory site by Mel Murray, author of "History of Fostoria, Ohio Glass," have turned up a considerable number of shards in this pattern.

However, the pattern was known to have been made for a considerable number of years, and it is likely that other companies may have handled some production of "Cosmos." It was reportedly also advertised by Westmoreland Specialty Glass Co., earlier this century. Whether they actually manufactured "Cosmos," and how they acquired the molds, is uncertain at this time. However, I have been told that "Cosmos" was given away as premiums for a time—which may explain the considerable availability of the pattern.

The man responsible for Cosmos was the brilliant and little-known Nicholas Kopp, Jr., a glass genius long-ignored by glass historians. Perhaps this series can remedy this unfortunate oversight. He headed the Consolidated factories for many years, but also headed production for Hobbs, Brockunier and Pittsburgh Lamp, Brass & Glass Companies. During his tenure, their production of colored glassware was altogether exciting.

Cosmos was not exclusively made in decorated milk glass. Rarely pieces are found in cased colors of pink, blue and yellow. These colors are definitely Consolidated (Kopp) colors, and are primarily found only in salt shakers and miniature lamps. Any other item in these colors should be considered rare.

Two similar patterns are sometimes confused for Cosmos. Primarily, the line known as "Apple Blossom" is responsible for a majority of the confusion. It has the same netted background, the same 5-petal flower, and similar color decoration. However, the patterns are distinctly different. The next installment in this series (in two weeks) will offer some startling information on this "Apple Blossom" line. Also of similar design, but seldom confused with "Cosmos," is the "Coreopsis" pattern. It lacks the netted background, is sometimes satin finished, and frequently has applied metal rims and tops.

SOME OF THE CONSOLIDATED'S TRADE MAKERS

02G.
Made in Rose and Yellow. Cased colors. Glaze and Satin Finish.

DAISY.
Assorted Decorations, and in Cased Colors.

800.
Made in Rose and Yellow. Cased Colors. Glaze and Satin Finish.

FIGURE A — A 1902 ad reprint of the Consolidated Lamp & Glass Company, of Coraopolis, Pa. It reveals the original name for the "Cosmos" pattern was "Daisy." On the left is the "Pansy" pattern miniature lamp. On the right, the "Cone" pattern.

"THE CROESUS PATTERN"
An Exposé on Something New

Only a limited number of pressed glass patterns have reached the height of collectibility and value of Riverside Glass Company's "Croesus". It was very popular at the time of its introduction in 1897, so there seems to be no shortage of pieces to satisfy the appetites of hundreds of collectors. Certain pieces are very rare, especially the celery, the jelly compote and the tiny individual serving pieces. Yet it is fortunate for the throngs of devoted collectors that the pattern is at least still available. Some patterns (and certain colors) are so very hard to find that "collecting" them is a hopeless venture.

The premium value of this pattern now finds itself threatened by an epidemic of reproductions which are literally flooding the antiques market. They are not being advertised in trade papers as new collectibles, they are not marked or identified by their makers in any way (not even a paper label), nor do they appear (to date) in a catalogue available to the public. This is nothing short of a deliberate attempt to secretly dupe the antique-buying public, and this article will attempt to prevent this criminal action from ever victimizing you.

To date, the pattern is being reproduced in the toothpick (since 1973), the covered butter (1974), and reports are now coming in that the entire table set (creamer, sugar, spooner, butter) is being imported from Japan, and yet another company is making a new tumbler. All are being made in very good colors of emerald green and amethyst (with gold), but I am told the table set is also available in crystal.

However, since the reports on the table set and tumblers are unconfirmed (but from a reliable source), I must limit this report to the details involving the new toothpick holders and butters which are peppering auctions, flea markets, and antiques shows throughout the country. Many collectors and dealers know about these reproductions, but surprisingly, almost as many do not. But one thing is certain; most do not know how to tell the difference between the old and new Croesus. Thus, this report.

The reproduction toothpick holders are good, but there are differences. Figure A and B reveal the easiest way to differentiate. *The tiny scroll at the top of the pattern does not curl all the way under on the new as it does on the old.* Another way to tell is to check the gold. *The gold on the new is decorated sloppily,* and is even rubbed off in spots to simulate age wear (another *deliberate* attempt to fool the public). The gold on the old is evenly decorated, and is worn (if at all) naturally and smoothly.

The suggested retail value of these new toothpicks is kept relatively high ($25), which is obviously meant to give these toothpicks a nerve-wracking "Sleeper" appeal when they are found by unsuspecting buyers at flea markets and auctions. The actual value of the original (old) Croesus toothpicks is as high as $100. Thus, the astronomical difference of $75 represents to this author a crime which deserves to be exposed to the public. However, legal repercussions make it impossible for me to name these glass wizards who have the power to devalue the investments of all glass collectors.

Last year, due to the success of the new toothpick, another company quietly released a new Croesus covered butter, which is certainly taking its toll of victims. It is a new mold, but it is good—*too* good! The retail value here is also relatively high ($40), and since the value of the old is as high as $150, few dealers and collectors can resist the temptation to invest in these very convincing reproductions. This difference in value of $110, and the fact that these butters were so secretly introduced, makes this an atrocity of even higher proportions than the toothpick.

Figure C illustrates an old Croesus butter next to a new. They appear identical at first glance, but luckily these butters are produced from a newly carved mold, so there *are* differences. *The finial on the old dome has uncurved sections forming the fan-like knob, while the new finial is taller and the sections are curved—more noticeable at the sides. The bottom rim of the dome lid on the old is gently rounded, but is flat and sharp-edged on the new.* Also, the outside scalloped edge of the old butter base is well-rounded and smooth, whereas the new butter bases often have an extra rim of glass projecting out (See Fig. D). The poorly executed gold decoration, with deliberate smearing to simulate wear, also applies to the butter.

As long as these and other reproductions continue to be a profitable venture, then collectors will continue to be threatened with the secretive appearance of more and more of these abominations. How many thousands of people will have their hard-earned money wasted on these reproductions before government legislation is passed requiring some form of permanent trademark? Certainly the handful of people responsible for these new pieces of glass do not have the power or the influence to prevent passage of such a bill. Their voice would be a whisper compared to the fury of antique glass investors who have been or are fearful of being "stung" by the new reproduction pattern glass.*

FIGURE A—Scroll design on OLD Croesus toothpick.

FIGURE B—Scroll design on NEW Croesus toothpick (taken from pencil rubbing, so there may be SLIGHT differences).

FIGURE C—(Left) Old Croesus Butter; (Right) New Croesus.

FIGURE D—(Left) Old Croesus Butter Base; (Right) New Butter Base

*An almost perfect tumbler has been reproduced by Mosser in all colors, unmarked of course.

41

"CRYSTAL WEDDING"

In the December, 1978, issue of *Glass Review,* staff writer Bea Senf featured a covered compote in a pattern she called "Wedding Bowl." Perhaps this is the pattern name used by Westmoreland Glass, but the catalogue reprint for the year 1891 shows that this line was originally called "Crystal Wedding," a name by which it is best known among pattern glass collectors.

"Crystal Wedding" was originally made by Adams & Company of Pittsburgh, Pa. It is rather notable that no covered compotes appeared in the early catalogue, but I cannot say without reservations that one was never made before 1900. The compote shown in Bea's column is undoubtedly a reissue by Westmoreland Glass, and as she states, it is still being made today.

The reprint here states the line was originally made in "plain, banded, frosted or engraved" crystal. It was also made in ruby-stained crystal and is rarely seen in cobalt blue. The ruby on the old glass is a deep red; the ruby on the reissues is not as rich and usually has iridescent highlights when reflected in the light. The pieces found with pink staining are not original and date from the last twenty years.

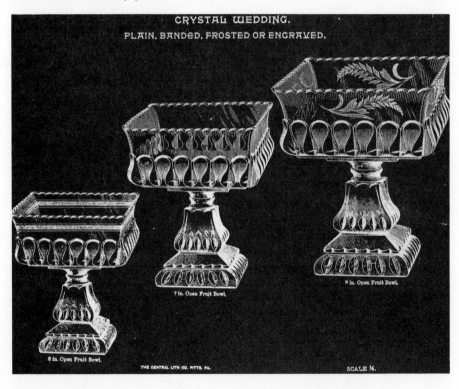

CRYSTAL WEDDING.
PLAIN, BANDED, FROSTED OR ENGRAVED.

6 in. Open Fruit Bowl.

7 in. Open Fruit Bowl.

8 in. Open Fruit Bowl.

THE CENTRAL LITH CO. PITTS. PA.

SCALE ⅓.

"DAISY & FERN" or "SPANISH LACE"?

Attribution of mold-blown opalescent patterns is certainly no simple task. These patterns are frequently overlooked in existing books on pattern identification which lean almost exclusively to the pressed varieties. Thus with no substantial reference material available, many of these blown patterns are known by so many names that confusion is rampant and collectibility is minimized.

One such pattern is "Daisy & Fern." Almost nothing has been offered previously regarding its origins, so I undertook considerable research to accurately report its maker in my book. After a detailed study of dozens of pieces of this pattern, the conclusion was that it was made by no less than three different glass companies, all from the Wheeling, W.Va. area.

However, before reporting just who made "Daisy & Fern," it should be determined just exactly which pattern it is. I have heard it called "Spanish Lace" so many times (Mrs. Taylor unfortunately documents this misconception in her sugar shaker book) that I have reprinted here a line drawing of the difference. Figure A illustrates the featured pattern, while Figure B shows us the similar, but distinctly different, "Spanish Lace" pattern. Figure C is the "Opalescent Seaweed" pattern which is likewise confused with "Spanish Lace." However, since we are concerned here with "Daisy & Fern," I will limit reporting my findings to the Figure A pattern.

Blown opalescent glassware first started appearing around 1885, with production innovated by the brilliant craftsmen at Hobbs, Brockunier & Company of Wheeling. One of these men was the creative Harry Northwood. Mr. Northwood worked for or managed three other companies besides Hobbs in the next five years, and every one of them advertised whole new lines of "Venetian" opalescent glassware during his tenure. One of these firms was the Buckeye Glass Company of Martins Ferry, Ohio (across the river from Wheeling,) with whom Northwood was associated for many years. It was here that I feel "Daisy & Fern" was first designed and produced. However, Mr. Northwood opened his own factory while simultaneously managing Buckeye, so the pattern could easily have been "born" there.

The primary reason for the Northwood attribution can be seen through a study of Figures D and E. The "Daisy & Fern" sugar shaker was produced from the same exact mold used on the popular "Royal Ivy" pattern. The "Daisy & Fern" toothpick holder (top row, Fig. E), is in the same mold as Northwood's "Parian Swirl" (Kamm calls this "Parian Ruby".) Also, the cruet on the left and the pickle castor insert have a netted "Apple blossom" mold, which I am certain is a Northwood creation. I will report my findings on this "Apple Blossom" pattern in a later installment in this series.

It is a known fact that blown opalescent patterns were copied by competitor factories in hopes of capturing a portion of their market. The "Coinspot" pattern can be found in a half-dozen different molds or shapes, these slight differences undertaken to avoid legal disputes. Besides the ribbed swirl and netted "Apple Blossom" molds, "Daisy & Fern" can also be found in the West Virginia Glass Co.'s "Optic" mold. It is scarce in this shape, usually found only in a few table items like syrups, sugar shakers and salt & peppers. It is uncertain why this glass company made "Daisy & Fern," but it is of interest that the head of West Virginia Glass, Hanson E. Waddell, was earlier associated with Hobbs, Brockunier. Perhaps this association directly influenced the production undertaken at his own firm.

Primary colors made were opalescent crystal, cranberry, and blue. It is scarcely found in canary yellow and is rare in green. Whether Buckeye, Northwood or West Virginia Glass, "Daisy & Fern" is a charming pattern which deserves to stand on its own, and should not be confused with other opalescent blown patterns.

Reproductions in cranberry are being massively produced today by L. G. Wright Glass Co., New Martinsville, W.Va. Shapes include a water pitcher (beware of reeded handles,) milk pitcher, tall creamer, tumbler (thick,) cruet (avoid tri-cornered spouts,) syrup (reeded handle,) sugar shaker ("Nine Panel" thick top rim,) barber bottle (melon ribbed,) pickle castor inserts, and several sizes of lamps and shades. All of the satin pieces found today are reproductions. I have been told that the pattern was reproduced in the thirties, but this has not been confirmed by this author, and I hesitate even mentioning it here.

 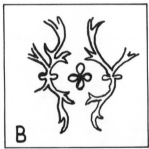 

Figure A—Daisy & Fern; Figure B—Spanish Lace; Figure C—Opalescent Seaweed.

Figure D—Daisy & Fern syrup in "Nine-Panel" mold.

Figure E—Spanish Lace spooner.

Figure E— (top row) "Parian Swirl" and "Daisy & Fern" toothpicks in same exact shapes; (row 2) "D & F" in "Apple Blossom" mold and another in the same mold as "Royal Ivy;" (bottom) "D & F" pickle castor, "Apple Blossom" mold, definitely Northwood.

THE "DELAWARE" & "BOHEMIAN" PATTERNS
Very Similar—But Distinctly Different

Sometimes when a pattern introduced by a glass company met with tremendous sales response, one of two things occurred. Most often a competitor would design a pattern mold strikingly similar, but just different enough to avoid legal infringements. However less often the same company would attempt to repeat its own success by creating another line with familiar pattern characteristics.

This week I will attempt to clear up some confusion concerning two patterns released by the U.S. Glass Company at the turn of the century, and present new information about them not available in existing glass literature. One of these is the popular "State" pattern, *Delaware,* shown here in a rare reprint from a U.S. Glass catalogue. The similar "sister" pattern, shown in Figure B, was originally called their *Bohemian* line. However, the name "Florodora" seems to have caught on among glass collectors (more on that matter later).

Careful study of the two patterns reveals obvious differences which make one wonder why dealers continue to confuse *Bohemian* for *Delaware.* Perhaps it is because both have the "Four Petal Flowers"—the name earlier tagged on *Delaware* before Kamm turned up the original name. Both also have foliage and berries. Both were made in identical colors (with minor exceptions), but this is where the similarity ends. *Delaware* has a border at the top and bottom of the pattern unlike the scrolly design found on *Bohemian.* However, the biggest difference, and by far the simplest way to tell the two patterns apart, is that all pieces of *Bohemian* (except the covered butter and tumblers) are footed, and *Delaware* is never footed.

Delaware was made in a wide variety of shapes, a testament to its extreme popularity. Introduced in 1900, its production continued for almost another decade (the catalogue from which the reprint was taken is dated 1909). Most of the shapes this pattern can be found in are well known. This would include the 4-piece table set, the water set, berry set (2 different shapes), cruet, celery vase, salt shakers, custard cup (often incorrectly called a punch cup), breakfast creamer and open sugar, finger bowl, toothpick holder and a tankard pitcher (called a claret jug in the catalogue). Less frequently seen is the dresser set, consisting of a puff box, a pomade box, a dresser tray, a pin tray and a ring tray; also a tall vase, a milk-size pitcher, and both miniature and full-size bride's baskets in two different shapes.

Bohemian was made in the 4-piece table set, water set, berry set, celery, toothpick, salt shaker, cologne bottle, covered soda straw holder, a tankard syrup pitcher (illustrated), a large round centerpiece bowl (looks almost like a large planter), and a breakfast size creamer and open sugar. No cruet has been documented in *Bohemian* to date. It most certainly would be extremely rare if it does exist.

An original advertisement featuring the *Bohemian* pattern is shown in Kamm 6, plate 59. It is from this ad that the other name, "Florodora," sprang up. The ad states "Write to us for cuts of Florodora, the latest decoration; found only on our #15063 *Bohemian* Pattern." Sounds simple enough, except for the fact that the ad prominently features the name of the decoration in large boldface type, with the name of the pattern lost in the fine print. Perhaps the reason the name *Bohemian* has met with such resistance is that it is confusing (a popular European etched ruby ware is known by the same name), and the name *Florodora* is much more attractive and exotic.

No matter what the pattern is called, it is just recently coming into its own, after years and years of "second class" stature among dealers and collectors. *Bohemian* has been overshadowed by *Delaware's* popularity and value for some time now, and yet it is much scarcer than *Delaware.* With collectors beginning to appreciate this rarity, prices are becoming comparable.

Both patterns can be found in crystal, emerald green, rose-flashed cranberry, and in crystal with color-stained flowers and leaves. All of these were usually gilded beautifully, but this gold is sometimes faded or completely missing from repeated washings over the years.

Delaware was also made in limited quantities in milk glass and in an ivory colored glass which resembles custard glass. This ivory color was created by U.S. Glass to compete with the popular custard glass after 1900 but it contains no uranium and lacks custard's luminous qualities. Only a few items in these colors are known—this writer having seen only the

FIGURE A—Reprint from 1909 U.S. Glass Company catalogue. Note the tankard shape pitcher was called a "claret jug."

creamer, tumbler, small berry dishes, breakfast creamer and sugar, and the three dresser trays. Any other piece in ivory would be quite rare.

Bohemian was also made in a frosted camphor-like crystal decorated with color on the leaves and flowers. It is most attractive in this color, with the combination of color and frosting unlike any other in recollection.

Fortunately, to date neither of these patterns has been plagued by reproductions. Both represent a safe and wise investment for any beginning or advanced collector of fine colored pattern glass.

FIGURE B—Scarce "Bohemian" pattern tankard syrup pitcher.

"DIAMOND BRIDGES"

In my Book 5, I named a pattern DIAMOND BRIDGES (Figure 240), listing it only in crystal and emerald green. Here are illustrated a very rare creamer and covered sugar in this pattern, with alternating panels of ruby-stain and frosting. I can think of no other pattern which utilizes this same combination of two decorating techniques. It is popular in amber-stained patterns, notably KLONDYKE, ZIPPER SLASH and the RIBBED DROPLET BAND pictured in this column earlier this year. DIAMOND BRIDGES was made by U.S. Glass Company, listed previously as their No. 15040 pattern, so I gave it a name for collectors. Little did I know then it would prove to be such an important pattern.

THE "DIAMONDS & CLUBS" PATTERN

This week I will be introducing to many of you a pattern which to date has remained unlisted in every major glass publication. I withheld this column for some time, hoping that additional documentation concerning its origins would turn up through my research, but decided to go ahead and present my "theories" and suffer the consequences should my attribution be proved incorrect at a later date. Should this occur, I will gladly print a retraction.

In offering these theories, I cannot stress enough the importance that they be interpreted by my readers as just that—theories. I am not attempting to set myself up as the final authority in this field, and indeed look forward to any documentation which might prove my presumptions to be inaccurate. I realize I am sticking my neck out at times, and there seems to be no shortage of critics willing to chop it off, but glass research is filled with thousands of voids which need to be filled. Remember, do not accept my theories as final proof of pattern origin—interpret them as educated theories.

I am calling this pattern *Diamonds & Clubs* since it has not been named before. It is a rather busy, later Victorian pattern, dating around 1910. The pattern on the water pitcher shown consists of a dizzy concoction of effects in basketweave, waves, daisies, diamonds, clubs and a central spade-like figure. However, only the diamonds and clubs appear on all pieces of this pattern, whereas the other motifs are usually missing. Thus, the origin of the name *Diamonds & Clubs*.

The pattern has been documented to date in the water pitcher, tumblers, a wine decanter and tiny wine glasses. I have not witnessed any other pieces, but will not rule out the possible existence of a table set or berry set.

Diamonds & Club can be found in emerald green, cobalt blue and in a very rare cranberry—all usually decorated with bright fired-on gold. However, this gold seems to be highly susceptible to fading and is sometimes partially missing. All pieces are very light in weight, obviously of the mold blown variety, and the handles on the pitcher and decanter are applied.

Recently a rare find turned up in this pattern. It was a lovely blue opalescent *Swastika* water pitcher in the *Diamonds & Clubs* mold. This is undoubtedly an experimental piece, which I consider myself fortunate to have even studied. Experimental pieces in carnival glass may also have been made.

Which brings us to attributing this pattern, which I am basing on the rather risky foundation of studying pattern, color and glass characteristics. Perhaps you will agree with my conclusions once they are presented in their entirety, and not as individual theories.

I strongly feel that *Diamonds & Clubs* was made by the Dugan Glass Company of Indiana, Pennsylvania. After 1913 it was called the Diamond Glass-Ware Company.

A modified version of the diamonds and clubs motif, as well as the double-bar border can be found on the *Diamond Maple Leaf* pattern, which is frequently found with Dugan's "D-in-a-Diamond" trademark. This trademark has inaccurately been attributed to a Canadian glass manufacturer, a growing presumption I wish once-and-for-all would be abolished.

It is also conclusive that both of these patterns can be found in identical shades of emerald green and cobalt blue (with gold), and both are unusually light-weight.

Several dozen shards in the popular *Spanish Lace* pattern have been unearthed recently at the factory dump site of the old Indiana, Pa., factory. The syrup pitcher for *Spanish Lace* and *Opalescent Swastika* are identical in shape, and undoubtedly from the same mold. Thus, they apparently had common manufacturers. Since *Diamonds & Clubs* was also made in a *Swastika* variant, this offers additional foundation for attribution.

For some time now, I have been stating that, although Northwood was no longer operating the Indiana, Pa., factory after he departed in 1902, he left the firm with considerable influence merely by having associated with the personnel. The Dugan Glass Company was named after and partially owned by Northwood's uncle, Thomas E. Dugan. I now have proof that Northwood's wife owned stock in the Dugan firm and that indeed Harry Northwood himself was *directly* involved in production and design at his former Pennsylvania location. This rather interesting quote was found by me in a 1905 trade journal,

"He (Northwood) says that his 'babies,' the plants at Indiana, Pa., Steubenville, Ohio, Martins Ferry, Ohio, and elsewhere, keep him busy in thinking about new designs and methods for selling his wares."

This quote is my long hoped-for proof that Northwood was perhaps the single most influential individual in the production of colored tableware from 1885 to 1920. It also provides the long-sought link between the Northwood and Jefferson Glass Companies, and the occasional mysterious overlap in their production of identical patterns.*

Thus, I can at least present the theory here that *Diamonds & Clubs* was most decidedly designed and produced with the distinctive "Northwood touch."

From another point of view, it is possible this quote means that the companies spawned by Northwood kept him busy thinking of new ideas to keep one jump ahead of the competitors.

"Diamonds & Clubs" water pitcher and wine glass.

"DIAMOND LIL"

Another unlisted pattern! There seems to be no end to them. Of the estimated 5,000 different patterns made in glass tableware sets, less than half have been properly attributed. By this I mean that the company and date of manufacture are known. Of the remaining two to three thousand, about a third have not even been named in the pioneer references on pattern glass. Thus we find almost a thousand patterns out here amongst us, sitting on flea market tables and on antiques shop shelves, just waiting to be officially christened.

Featured this month is a pattern shown here (figure A) in a spooner, covered sugar and creamer. At a quick glance, one would assume it to be the *Panama* pattern, made by U.S. Glass. But a careful comparison to the spooner (Figure B) proves the two patterns are only similar. I scanned the works of Kamm, Metz and Lee carefully to find the name of this line and came up with a big zero.

The ad was found in a glass industry trade journal from early 1904, which identifies this pattern as the National Glass Company's #913. Since most collectors prefer a pattern name over a company number, I am taking the liberty of dubbing this pattern DIAMOND LIL. The design is a variation of the popular "strawberry and fan" motif found on dozens of pressed and cut glass patterns.

Not much is known about this pattern at this time, but it probably was made only in crystal, as I have not seen it in any color to date. *Diamond Lil* was undoubtedly made only for a limited time, since the National Glass Company disbanded a few months after the appearance of this ad.

Diamond Lil was probably also made in a covered butter, which would complete the four-piece table set, a water set and berry set. I have never seen a toothpick holder, cruet or syrup pitcher, but they are also likely. The pattern has never been reproduced and represents a good investment now that its origins are known and collectibility is certain to increase.

NO. 913. SPOON, SUGAR AND CREAM. BY THE NATIONAL GLASS CO., PITTSBURG.

FIGURE A—Spooner, sugar and creamer in previously unlisted DIAMOND LIL pattern, circa 1904.

No. 15088. Spoon. From the United States Glass Co., Pittsburg, Pa.

FIGURE B—Spooner in similar PANAMA pattern, reprinted from November, 1904 trade journal.

"DIAMOND PYRAMIDS"
An Unlisted Fostoria Pattern

As I sit and ponder at my desk wondering which column to write next, or which glass pattern will interest my readers most, I frequently shake my head in realization of how little I really do know. And as I dig through the mountains of files built up over the past few years, I shudder to think that I may be passing over a very important piece of information. It awes me to think that what I know now is only a fraction of what I will know in another decade.

Illustrated here is a pattern which was produced in early 1902 by the Fostoria Glass Company of Moundsville, West Virginia. The reprint is from an issue of the "China, Glass and Pottery Review." I must have skimmed past the page on which this creamer appeared a dozen times or more. It looked so familiar I figured it *had* to be listed *somewhere* in Kamm.

Then one day, while I was researching another pattern for this column, I came across this creamer again just minutes after I had checked the clear pattern glass section of my book, "1,000 Toothpick Holders." It was like a bolt of electricity went through me when I noticed that the toothpick I named "Inverted Imperial" was one and the same.

I checked the two existing books on early Fostoria glass and this pattern was nowhere to be found. I have in my files an 1899 catalogue by Fostoria Glass, and a 1901 and 1903 catalogue were reprinted in the two books. Apparently this creamer was part of a new line in 1902, didn't sell very well, and failed to appear in the 1903 catalogue.

This leads us to the problem of a name for this pattern. I called it "Inverted Imperial" in my toothpick book because of the strong similarity to the Imperial Glass Company's #9 pattern (shown in Kamm 7, plate 82.) I knew they weren't the same design but I suspected the same maker was responsible for both. Thus, the name *Inverted Imperial,* which now seems inappropriate and confusing.

I only condone name changes on patterns when the original manufacturer's name is discovered or when the present name proves confusing to collectors. In this case, I am calling this pattern *DIAMOND PYRAMIDS* because it is not well-known enough yet as "Inverted Imperial" to cause too much confusion with a name change. To continue with the old name now would imply that Imperial Glass had something to do with its creation, which it did not.

Diamond Pyramids was made in Fostoria's usual wide variety of shapes, table set, water set, berry set, assorted bowls and nappies, salt shaker, toothpick holder, celery vase, etc. It was made in clear glass only, of good quality crystal.

It is really exciting to come up with "exclusives" like this. The field of pattern glass is a massive one, involving thousands of patterns made in tens of thousands of different shapes. It's a big job, too big for one person. The biggest pleasure I get from research is sharing my findings. I look forward to other collectors getting involved in this wide open field and publishing their findings. One such individual is J. Chris Ramsey from Maryland, with whom I must share this discovery, as it was through his efforts at the Library of Congress that this long-lost Fostoria ad was re-discovered. I want to thank him again for sending photo-copies of glass journals which make important reports like this possible.

Diamond Pyramid creamer.

"DIAMOND SPEARHEAD"
At Last the Answer is Known!

This week I will re-introduce many of you to a pattern which has until recently been overlooked by virtually every collector, dealer and glass historian. It seems unbelievable that it remained unlisted until 1970, when Dr. Peterson included an example (and provided the name) in his book on salt shakers. This pattern, called *Diamond Spearhead,* has been avoided by most collectors, undoubtedly due to the fact that so little has been reported about it until now.

It is incredible that this pattern escaped the attention of our glass research pioneers. It is by no means a rare pattern, although certain items are very scarce (including the illustrated covered butter). *Diamond Spearhead* is made in a complete table service, in opalescent colors of canary yellow, green, white, and two shades of blue—cobalt and sapphire blue.

Considerable effort has been expended in tracing down this pattern's origins. I have not been able to turn up any old catalogues or trade journal advertisements. A study of color and pattern characteristics only proved baffling. In my first book, I based my attribution upon the spring lid to the syrup jug in this pattern, which is identical to others found on patterns made "under the Northwood influence." A rather weak attribution, I realize—but I hated to be any more definite with my claim when the pattern and colors were so unlike anything else Northwood had ever done. By the time my second volume was released, I was more inclined to believe the pattern was made by Jefferson or McKee Glass, primarily because of the similarity in color to their known patterns.

It is with great pleasure that now I can print a retraction to my incorrect conclusion from Book 2. Knowing the answer to this plaguing question and reporting it in this column is far more important than the discredit it brings my earlier report. I can now report to you where *Diamond Spearhead* was made.

You will note I say "where" it was made. Two weeks ago I told you about the extreme privilege I was granted in getting a chance to rummage through several boxes of glass shards which were uncovered at the Indiana, Pennsylvania factory site where the old Northwood Company once stood. Boxes and boxes of these shards were sent to me for study, and it is impossible for me to relate here what a thrill it was sifting through the past, and reconstructing the long-lost history of this proud factory.

The man who is responsible for sending these thousands of pieces of glass to me can never be thanked enough. Each time a trench was dug, a flower bed upturned, even a hole dug for a stop sign, this man would be out there with his bucket, picking up every tiny sliver of glass that might prove important. Many of these shards were common knowledge, known Northwood patterns like *Intaglio, Chrysanthemum Sprig,* and *Fluted Scrolls.* But there were many shards from patterns which were completely uncredited to Northwood, and to this researcher it brings great pride to be the one who discloses the names of these patterns. But I humbly take second credit to the man who made all this possible through his unparalleled dedication and priceless help offered, which thus improved the status of pattern glass documentation for future generations.

To this writer, finding two shards of *Diamond Spearhead* among all those others was much like the feeling we all have when we uncover a "sleeper" in a junk shop, or that long-sought item which completes a set. Both of these pieces were in canary and were large enough to distinguish the pattern easily. A line drawing of one of these is presented here.

Yet this most important discovery is only half complete. For you see, Harry Northwood sold his holdings in this factory around 1902. After that, production was continued by National Glass (still retaining the Northwood factory name until 1904) and then by the Dugan Glass Works (later called the Diamond Glass Company). The plant continued to operate until June, 1931 when the factory burned to the ground.

Without some way to date the pattern definitely it is difficult to tell for certain whether *Diamond Spearhead* was made before or after Northwood's departure. The major problem in attributing some of these shards is trying to decipher the "transitional" patterns—those which were made shortly after Northwood pulled out. The only possible dating procedure is to find the pattern illustrated in a Montgomery Wards or Butler Brothers catalogue. The *Nestor* pattern was advertised in 1903, after Northwood left the firm, but the factory workers all retained the distinguishable Northwood "touch" and the company retained most of the market which had been built up over the years by its previous owner.

For the benefit of those who collect Northwood glass, and not the products of his offsprings, I will attempt to pinpoint the date of production of *Diamond Spearhead* without the aid of any catalogue listings.*

Diamond Spearhead was produced in a tremendous variety of shapes, surpassed only by one other opalescent pattern, *Beatty Ribbed Opal*. It can be found in a 4-piece table set (butter, creamer, sugar, spooner), a water set (tumblers and/or goblets), a berry set, celery vase, toothpick holder, salt shakers, a syrup jug, an individual creamer and open sugar, a mug (or custard cup), a jelly compote and I just recently witnessed the existence of a beautiful high-standard open compote.* These many items lead me to believe the pattern dates prior to Northwood's departure. After 1900 the number of shapes offered in a pressed glass table service was fewer and fewer until, by 1905, if more than eight items were made it was rare indeed.

It is confusing, however, that the existence of a cruet in *Diamond Spearhead* cannot be confirmed. If it does exist, I certainly would like to hear from the lucky owner so the piece can be documented.

The color most often seen is the canary opalescent. The rarest and, by far, most attractive color is the cobalt blue opalescent. I have been told that "Iris with Meader" had been made in this unusual opalescent color, and this report led me to my previous incorrect conclusion that Jefferson Glass may have created *D.S.* I detest depending upon heresay for my research, but unfortunately it is every historian's downfall.

At the present time, the value of *Diamond Spearhead* is lower than practically all other opalescent patterns. Perhaps with this report, these values will increase proportionately with the others, for *Diamond Spearhead* stands on its own in this field.

A mug has been found, souvenir dated 1900. See next page.
Also known in a rare water bottle, cake plate, breakfast creamer & sugar.

Line drawing of shard unearthed from a Diamond Spearhead water pitcher.

Souvenir mug in Diamond Spearhead, dated 1900.

Diamond Spearhead jelly compote.

"DICE & BLOCK"

One of the biggest thrills for a glass researcher is when a long-lost catalogue surfaces or when pattern glass shards are unearthed at an old factory site long since forgotten.

In the past month, I have been extremely honored by having been given the opportunity to study a company catalogue (circa 1885) of the old Belmont Glass Company of Bellaire, Ohio. I was also fortunate enough to sift through literally hundreds of pieces of glass recently dug up at Northwood's Indiana, Pennsylvania factory site, where a university football field rests today.

Both of these privileges were granted by individuals who have thus provided some priceless documentation which will not gather dust wastefully in their closet, but which can now be shared with thousands of readers who look to this column for updated information on pattern glass.

Illustrated here is a deep amber cruet which can be found in many cruet collections across the country. It is included in Murray's first book on cruets—he calls it "Dice & Block"—but not in his second. The pattern appears nowhere else, which aroused my curiosity concerning its origins for quite some time.

Glass enthusiasts can imagine my delight when I came across this cruet, illustrated in the referred to Belmont catalogue as their Number 101 pattern.*

To avoid confusion with the popular and highly collectible *Belmont #100* pattern, I believe the Murray name "Dice & Block" should be used hereafter.

The most intriguing feature about this pattern is that the cruet is the only shape illustrated in #101 in the catalogue. The likelihood is strong that this is the only shape available. This would easily explain why it was never listed by earlier researchers, as Kamm stuck primarily to pitchers, Metz and Millard to goblets, and Lee to patterns made in sets. If *Dice & Block* was indeed only made in a cruet, then it would understandably have escaped the attention of the pioneers in this field.

Made in colors of deep amber, pale blue, canary and crystal, the stopper illustrated is original. If table setting pieces like goblets, pitchers or compotes *were* made, then I will be documenting these pieces later as I continue my reports on other patterns shown in this priceless Belmont Glass Company catalogue.

As for the Northwood shards, I have some rather startling announcements for you there too. Many patterns which were merely listed by myself and others as "possibly Northwood" can now be positively documented. Also, there were dozens of carnival glass shards among these pieces, which means the often overlooked Dugan Glass Company, which took over the Northwood factory in 1903, undoubtedly can be added to the limited list of producers of iridescent glassware. More on this in a later installment.

Dice and Block cruet in amber.

*Dice & Block was also made by McKee Glass, circa 1885. Apparently the molds were sold from one to the other.

"THE DOUGLASS PATTERN"

Certainly one of the most popular *types* of colored glass isn't actually colored glass at all. Color-stained glass is in reality a fully formed base piece of crystal which is hand-decorated, dipped or washed in a bath of color staining, and then re-fired for permanence. The popular ruby-stained glass is one form of this "colored" glass. This technique was also used in coloring glass shades of amber to yellow (i.e. the Frances Ware line), a deep rose or cranberry color (popular in the *Delaware* pattern), and varying other shades from amethyst to green.

This week I will be discussing an unlisted pattern (in existing glass literature) shown here in a rather scarce ruby-stained water pitcher shown as Figure A. This pitcher was seen in an antiques show and, when queried, the dealer exhibiting the piece said he was unable to find the pattern name anywhere. I asked if I could photograph the piece for possible future listing, and the dealer graciously complied.

It was with some excitement that I turned up the Figure B advertisement which indeed identifies the pattern of the water pitcher as "Douglass Ware." I found the ad in the archives of the Ohio State University Library in an April, 1903 issue of "Illustrated Glass & Pottery World." The pattern was made by the Co-operative Flint Glass Company of Beaver Falls, Pa.

Douglass resembles any number of "Colonial" type patterns, especially in the illustrated covered butter at the top of the ad. It seems that just about every glass company existing after 1900 produced a simple panelled pattern which they could sell cheaply to hotels and restaurants and peddle as premium ware to retail merchants. Northwood's is known as "Flute". Heisey, Jefferson and U.S. Glass assigned numbers to theirs. The distinction *Douglass* has over these others is that it bulges out slightly at the bottom, just before forming a pedestalled base. The exceptions to this pattern characteristic are the aforementioned covered butter (a pedestal-based butter is also shown in Figure B), the tumbler and the toothpick holder (see Figure C).

The water pitcher illustrated has an attractive etched design of Fleur-de-Lis on each of the six panels. The toothpick holder is not etched. The other known items include the 4-piece table setting (creamer, covered sugar, spooner and the two different covered butters), the tumbler, berry set, and a salt shaker. Other likely pieces would include the celery vase and perhaps a covered compote. The glass is very heavy and thick, and appears to be of much earlier vintage than its 1903 production date.

No cruet, jelly compote or goblets have been reported or seen by this writer to date. They will be listed in a later column should their existence be verified.

FIGURE A—Rare ruby-stained Douglass pattern water pitcher with Fleur-de-Lis etching.

FIGURE C—Scarce ruby-stained toothpick
holder in the Douglass pattern.

FIGURE B—April, 1903 advertisement displaying "Douglass Ware"
table set. Note the two differently shaped covered butters.

"DUNCAN'S #42 PATTERN"

It is usually the case among glass researchers to name those patterns featured in their reports or publications. In a few early cases these patterns were named after the dealer from whom the example was purchased, or the collector who owned the item, or even the town in which it was found. This is a practice which Kamm justifiably condemned. She preferred to stick to original manufacturer's names or numbers—sometimes even when another name had reached public acceptance. It is unfortunate that the early works of Kamm, Lee and Millard often overlap in providing different names for identical patterns. It is even more unfortunate that the goblets illustrated in the later works of Metz and the Unitts endorsed the Millard names rather than those by Kamm (the most complete and documented pattern references available)—thus continuing confusion into presentday nomenclature.

It is unique in pattern glass annals that this week's featured pattern has reached considerable popularity, despite the fact that it is known only by the number of its manufacturer. This pattern is known today as "Duncan's #42"—or on occasion "D & M #42" (the initials stand for Duncan & Miller). Until now that pattern has been reported only in crystal—of superior quality, easily confused for cut glass when one is fortunate enough to see an entire collection.

Another pattern known only by a number, "King's #500" is sometimes called "Parrot"—which is incorrect since Kamm was referring to a figural parrot syrup pitcher which was advertised on the same page illustrating the "King's #500" table set. Collectors please take note of this commonly used misnomer.

Duncan's #42 was introduced by its maker in 1898, and was so popular that production was continued after the name of the firm was changed in 1901 from George Duncan's Sons & Co. to The Duncan & Miller Glass Co. See the Figure A ad reprint from a February, 1899 issue of "China, Glass & Pottery Review," which illustrates the creamer and covered sugar.

It is not well known that *Duncan's #42* can rarely be found in ruby-stained glass. Illustrated as Figure B is a water set in this scarce color decoration, which is etched "1899" on the tumblers. However the water pitcher is etched "Mr. & Mrs. Herman J. Bucher—Married Nov. 30, 1893." If the tumblers had become separated from the pitcher through succeeding generations, one might have been led to believe the tankard was made in 1893. However, I am fairly certain that this must have been an anniversary gift for the Bucher's sixth year of marriage. The tumblers have a monogrammed letter "B" on the reverse side.

Duncan's #42 can be found in a variant with thumbprints and slashes at the top of the zippered panels. I cannot imagine why Duncan put out this variation with the same number assigned to it.

Duncan's #42 was made in a tremendous variety of shapes and sizes, too many to mention here. In my last column (featuring Duncan's #52 pattern), I mentioned that the punch bowl, cup and underplate were reproduced in the 1940s in crystal, in both the #42 and #52 patterns. However, I just noticed that the catalogue from which I drew this information was issued in 1955, just prior to the closing of the Duncan & Miller factory. Otherwise, *Duncan's #42* is a relatively safe investment for collectors wishing to accumulate a pattern with limited reproduction pitfalls.

FIGURE A—February, 1899 advertisement featuring "Duncan's #42" pattern.

FIGURE B—A very rare ruby-stained "Duncan #42" water set, etch-dated "1899."

Recently the original Duncan name for this pattern, MARDIS GRAS, has achieved acceptance among collectors.

"ELEPHANT TOES"

Illustrated here is a four-piece table set in a pattern which before 1978 remained unlisted in modern glass literature. I pictured a toothpick holder in my book "1000 Toothpick Holders" in 1976; and, hard-pressed for a name for the pattern, named it ELEPHANT TOES because of the similarity of the toothpick to the lumbering foot of an elephant. This same similarity can be witnessed on the spooner shown here at the left.

Often I have been put into the position of guessing which company made a specific pattern, due to the fact that attribution cannot be confirmed by existing catalogues, trade journal advertisements or shard diggings. When this guesswork is forced upon me, I base attribution on the design and color of the glass. If I have serious doubts, I will state "maker unknown" or "maker uncertain." But on ELEPHANT TOES, I am almost positive that it was a pattern of the United States Glass Company. The large "thumbprints" along the base are sometimes found flashed with cranberry, amethyst or green color—identical in color and style to some pieces of *King's Crown, Manhattan, Galloway* and other known U.S. Glass patterns.

ELEPHANT TOES dates around 1905. I would be fascinated to find out if this pattern, or others I have attributed to U.S. Glass (*Double Dahlia with Lens, Bead & Scroll*) is perhaps one of the states for which we don't have a pattern, *Arkansas, Mississippi, Rhode Island* and *West Virginia*. Other states which joined the Union after 1900, Oklahoma, Arizona and New Mexico, probably didn't have the population to warrant having a state named after them. The last state pattern to be named was Washington in 1904.

ELEPHANT TOES can be found in a table set, water set, berry set, celery vase, toothpick holder, salt shaker and assorted nappies. Other items have not been confirmed to date. No reproductions have been introduced to confuse new collectors.

"THE EMPRESS PATTERN"
A Future Superstar in Collectible Pattern Glass

In these investment-conscious times, I am frequently asked what would be a good pattern to collect. There are so many possibilities that it is impossible for me to pinpoint just one pattern which would represent a good investment. I do believe that certain colored patterns like *Croesus, Holly Amber, Cosmos and Libbey's Maize* have reached a peak in value which has, and will continue to, remain stable for a while longer. But there are dozens of little-known patterns which have had their potential value hampered by one of three things — an improper (or lack of a) listing in Kamm, Metz or Lee, no maker being known, or a fear of reproductions. Because of recent research findings, I have seen patterns like *Leaf Mold, Everglades* and Leaf Medallion almost double their collectibility and value.

An educated buying public means a healthy market. My purpose in research (and subsequent reports through this column and my books) is not necessarily to add fuel to these mushrooming market tendencies. There are those who criticize and express fears that my research reports are making it almost impossible to find a decent bargain any more. I will not attempt to answer these accusations here in this column, but I will say that if this unfortunate after-effect of my work is true, then the advantages for the many far out-weigh the disadvantages to the few. These reports are adding a new vitality to a reproduction-plagued market.

This week's report concerns the *Empress* pattern, which is certainly not an "unknown." There are many facts concerning it which are well-known. Most collectors know it is a Riverside Glass pattern, the same firm which made the ever-popular *Croesus. Empress* is easily recognized in most pieces, and yet Kamm named it *Double Arch* in her Book 7 (unfortunately she called a different pattern the same name in Book 5). The reason for this double-name confusion is even harder to understand since the butter dish in *Empress* is illustrated in an ad reprint on pg. 200 of the same Book 7. She ironically states that the butter's pattern was "not shown in modern glass literature." This oversight was no doubt due to the fact that the "arches" are upside-down on several pieces of *Empress* — note the cruet and syrup illustrated here, as well as the butter dish shown in Kamm. Considering the monumental achievements of Mrs. Kamm in glass research, I consider this small error microscopic. It is virtually impossible to prepare a publication on early American glass free of mistakes. However, I wish the present editors of the priceless Kamm works would do credit to Mrs. Kamm's memory by updating her work with appropriate editorial notes — a practice I am certain our Minnie would have condoned.

The "Empress" name was the original manufacturer's name for this regal looking pattern. As previously stated, many facts concerning this pattern are common knowledge. But there are many which are not, and it is these little bits of unlisted data which I will concentrate on here.

Empress was primarily made in crystal (sometimes engraved) and in a deep emerald green, usually with gold. However, it is not well-known that a few experimental pieces were produced in the same brilliant amethyst which is so popular in Riverside's *Croesus*. Unfortunately, so little amethyst *Empress* was made that it is impossible to try to collect, and anyone who owns even a single piece can consider themselves most fortunate. In fact, this author has not yet even handled a single piece in this color, but I have received several bona-fide reports of its existence. I had hoped to locate a piece for illustration here, but luck has not been with me.

Most collectors of this pattern know most of the items *Empress* can be found in—the table set, water set, berry set, cruet, toothpick, syrup, jelly compote, high-standard compote, salt shaker and the extremely hard-to-find celery vase. But most of them are not even aware that *Empress* was also made in a small breakfast-size creamer and covered sugar, a covered mustard, and three different lamps (illustrated here). There was also a custard cup, which most times is incorrectly called a punch cup (no punch bowl was made).*

By far the least-known *Empress* pieces would be the tiny salt dip, the pickle dish and cruet-set tray. These pieces completely lack the "arches" which distinguish the pattern, but they have the pattern characteristics of the scroll-work found at the base of most pieces (see the berry bowl in Fig. A).

Other new bits of data: the lamps were made in crystal and green, but were not gold decorated. The arches lack the tiny notches found on the table items. Also, the berry set comes in two different shapes—as illustrated here, and in a flatter shape with ruffled edges, obviously the result of careful hand-work.

Empress is a pleasantly designed pattern without all the ornate frills found in the *Croesus* line. Its future appears bright as more and more collectors fall prey to its basic charms. Prices have been increasing rapidly this past year, and it makes me wonder if *Empress* could possibly catch up to the popularity of *Croesus*. It seems unlikely, but you must recall that *Croesus* is now undermined by a glut of almost perfect reproductions, whereas *Empress* is not. The new collectors joining our ranks every day are looking for a "safe" investment for their money, and it is difficult for the novices to distinguish the new from the old. With this in mind, I highly recommend *Empress* to those of you who want to get in on the ground floor of something big.

---

*The mustard to this set has a base very much like a custard cup, but it is taller and leaner in shape.

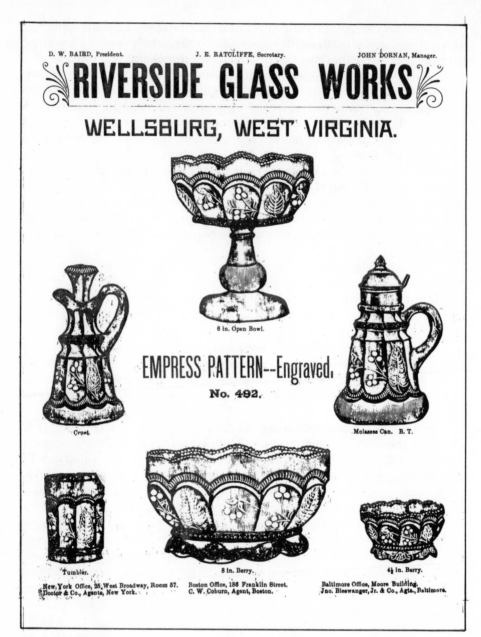

RIVERSIDE GLASS WORKS

WELLSBURG, WEST VIRGINIA.

6 in. Open Bowl.

EMPRESS PATTERN--Engraved.

No. 492.

Cruet.

Molasses Can. B. T.

Tumbler.

8 in. Berry.

4½ in. Berry.

Fig. A—Reprint of a February, 1899 advertisement illustrating several choice examples of the "Empress" pattern.

Fig. B—1899 advertisement illustrating three different lamps in the "Empress" pattern. Note the number of the pattern is different from the tableware items.

FOSTORIA'S "ERMINIE" PATTERN

Illustrated here is a little known, almost unlisted pattern made by the Fostoria Glass Company in 1898. The reprint shown is from a previously unpublished catalogue I have in my files, which contains many patterns and novelties not included in the two available catalogue reprints of Fostoria glass.

Weatherman does mention a #602 "Ermine" pattern, but according to the page shown here, the correct spelling is *Erminie*. The pattern did not appear in Fostoria's 1900 catalogue, so no illustration was available for the Weatherman reprint.

It is rather interesting to note that the creamer in *Erminie* is identical to the one used on the popular *St. Bernard* pattern made by Fostoria in 1895. In fact the base to the butter is the same on both patterns (see Kamm 5, plate 13). Perhaps in some sort of economy move the old *St. Bernard* molds were re-tooled to create a simpler finial. The finial on the earlier pattern is a rather detailed reclining dog.

According to this 1898 catalogue, *Erminie* was made in the table set shown here, a 4" and a 4½" nappy, a 6, 7 and 8" berry dish, several high and low-standard open compotes, the same in covered compotes, a 9" and 10" cake salver, an oil cruet, a syrup pitcher, a salt shaker, a celery vase, a pickle dish, an 8" oblong oval dish, and a celery tray. It is interesting to note that the catalogue and accompanying price list do not include a water set or toothpick holder in *Erminie*.

Also shown on the reprint here is a set of Fostoria's #600 *Brazilian,* which is an imitation cut pattern which is familiar to most pattern glass dealers and collectors. It has been well documented in the past by Kamm—in fact she listed it first in her Book 5 as "Cane Shield" and in her Book 7 by its original manufacturer's name, *Brazilian.*

Erminie and *Brazilian* were both made in crystal, with the latter also available in a rich emerald green. No reproductions are known in either pattern, so they represent a safe investment to collectors wary of reproductions.

ALL OUR WARE IS GOOD WEIGHT AND EXTRA FIRE POLISHED WITH NATURAL GAS, EXCEPT WHERE NOTED.

FOSTORIA GLASS CO., MOUNDSVILLE, W. VA.

SCALE, HALF SIZE.

Butter and Cover.
Packed 3¼ doz. in bbl.

Spoon.
Packed 8 doz. in bbl.

602 Erminie Set.

Packed 1½ doz. Sets in bbl.

Cream.
Packed 7 doz. in bbl.

Sugar and Cover.
Packed 4½ doz. in bbl.

Spoon.
Packed 8 doz. in bbl.

Cream.
Packed 8 doz. in bbl.

600 Brazilian Set.

Packed 1½ doz. Sets in bbl.

Butter and Cover.

Sugar and Cover.

"THE ESTHER PATTERN"

The Riverside Glass Works of Wellsburg, W.Va. has the distinction of having produced perhaps one of the most popular, collectible and now expensive patterns in pressed colored glass—"Croesus." So much has been written about this pattern that I am unable to offer anything new to its collectors—except perhaps that there are still a few who do not know that the toothpick and butter dish are being reproduced and are now flooding the market. (More regarding this matter in a late installment).

This week I will be offering some new information to the collectors of Riverside's less-revered, but still highly collectible "Esther" pattern. It may surprise you that many of this pattern's collectors started because their name (or their mother's name) was Esther. Certainly the pattern stands on its own merits. The pattern design is appealing without being too ornate and it is available in several different colors and decoration variants.

"Esther" is the original name for our featured pattern, although it is still sometimes referred to as "Tooth and Claw", primarily by goblet collectors. It was given a massive advertising build-up by Riverside when it was introduced by them, including a front page spread on the February 12, 1896 issue of "China, Glass & Lamps" (an early industry trade journal). This issue was found by me in the archives of a college library, and the cover is reprinted here for your enjoyment.

This reprint is of major interest because it reveals for the first time an unlisted item for the collectors of "Esther", a revolving caster set. The possible reason this piece has remained unlisted for so long in price guides and pattern glass volumes is undoubtedly due to the lack of the "teeth" and "claws" from the caster frame's design. Only the sunburst rays remain. However, close inspection of the oil bottle stopper reveals it to be exactly the same as the one used in the "Esther" oil cruet. The bottle inserts themselves lack any pattern characteristics at all, and it would undoubtedly be difficult for a collector to piece together a complete set because of this. A collector with a complete set can consider himself most fortunate, as this set is undoubtedly very rare, especially in emerald green or in color-stained crystal.

"Esther" was decorated at nearby Martins Ferry, Ohio by the Beaumont Glass Company, which had a large decorating staff. Beaumont also did the decorating for many of the patterns put out by McKee, such as "Feather" (Doric) and "Champion."

Besides crystal and emerald green, "Esther" is also available in ruby and amber-stained glass. The amber-staining can range from a pale yellow "wash" to a deep brown shade. This amber color was frequently enamel decorated with tiny little forget-me-nots.

"Esther" is reaching new heights of collectibility, probably due to the amazing level reached by Riverside's sister patterns, "Croesus" and "Empress." Another pattern produced by Riverside, the "X-Ray" line, is also coming into its own, despite its rather simple pattern design.

CHINA GLASS & LAMPS

VOL. XI. NO. 9.   PITTSBURGH, FEBRUARY 12, 1896. $2.00 PER ANNUM.

❧RIVERSIDE GLASS WORKS,❧

WELLSBURG, WEST VIRGINIA, U. S. A.

THE "ESTHER" REVOLVING CASTER.

YOUR JOBBER HANDLES THESE GOODS.

OUR LATEST AND BEST.   VERY PRETTY.   VERY RICH.

Complete line of samples now on exhibition at Wheeling Crockery, Glass and Lamp Exchange.

New York Representative, DOCTOR & CO,   Baltimore Representative, J. BEISWANGER, JR. & CO.

"EVERGLADES"—AN UPDATED REPORT

Once a pattern has been named by an author or historian of early glassware, and the name has been accepted for some time by collectors and dealers, it only proves confusing to introduce another name. It is with this in mind that I include this report in the series. I am not attempting to change the pattern's name—only report the original manufacturer's name and other data concerning the Northwood "Everglades" pattern.

Reprinted (Figure A) is a Northwood ad which I found in a 1902 trade journal, which offered no illustration or pattern characteristics to the announced "Carnelian" line. My curiosity aroused, I dug deeper through those crumbling journals, and was rewarded when I came across a full-page illustration of "H. Northwood & Co.'s brilliant 'Carnelian' ware." It is the pattern we know of today as "Everglades," and the page is reprinted for your enjoyment (Figure B).

Dr. Peterson, in his book on salt shakers, reports that this pattern was named "Everglades" by Robert Batty of Little Rock, Arkansas. I am not certain how or where Mr. Batty introduced this nomenclature, but the name apparently met with public favor. Neither Kamm nor Metz list this pattern, but Hartung includes it in her books on Northwood and opalescent glass. She refers to an early Northwood ad she is fortunate to own which apparently made no mention of the "Carnelian" name.

Introduced by Northwood in ivory ware (custard glass), production was apparently limited to the 1902-1903 season—shortly after the establishment of his new Wheeling, W.Va., factory (in the old Hobbs, Brockunier plant). "Everglades" is very popular in this custard color, and certain pieces (the cruet, salt & pepper) are considered extremely rare—commanding premium prices today. Also popular are pieces in opalescent colors of white, canary and blue. These are just as scarce as the custard line, which may explain why so few pattern glass books include them in their listings.

Opalescent pattern glass, which pre-dates the carnival era about ten years, is a fast-rising "star" in the collecting field—especially in the Northwood lines. His "Alaska," "Inverted Fan & Feather" and "Wild Bouquet" lines are already competitively priced with some of the choice carnival lines. It is only a matter of time before others meet this challenge. "Everglades" is among the "elite" already.

It is not well-known, however, that "Everglades" underwent limited production in opaque clambroth and purple slag. I have only seen salt shakers in these colors todate, but no doubt other items can be found in these rare colors.

In closing, I reiterate that it is not my intention to create confusion over the names of this pattern. As a glass historian, I felt it was merely of interest to other students and collectors. It is the duty of all researchers to share their findings with others. To hold back discoveries is simply criminal, and leaves unfortunate "voids" in a field desperately in need of more documentation.

FIGURE A. 1902 ad introducing the Carnelian line.

FIGURE B. Full page ad illustrating "Carnelian" Ware.

"GIBSON GIRL"—ANOTHER UPDATED REPORT

Unfortunately, this writer has a limited background in the field of pressed crystal. I have never made claims to have anything more than a working knowledge. However, when my research in the field of my first love, early colored pattern glass, turns up an important discovery in another field, then I consider it my duty to report these findings no matter how incomplete or awkward the results may be.

This week's featured pattern, known only in clear glass, is designed with such style and in such superior crystal that it appears to be of much earlier vintage than the actual year of production. Known today as "Gibson Girl" (Kamm 2, pg. 26), it was named by Mrs. Kamm due to the likeness of the cameo figure to the unmistakable look of the central character of illustrator Charles Dana Gibson. Both Kamm and Metz date this glass shortly after 1900, coinciding with the height of Mr. Gibson's popularity.

This presumption can now be confirmed, as the illustrated advertisement dates the "Gibson Girl" line, introduced in December, 1903. Until now, no maker has been reported. However, you can now see that it was announced by the National Glass Company, with production taking place at their Keystone Tumbler Works of Rochester, Pennsylvania. It was originally named the "Medallion" pattern by its maker. It would only prove confusing to re-introduce this name today, as there is another well-known pattern listed by that name.

Very little is known about the company which made this pattern. It was established in 1897, and apparently closed down (or was shut down) shortly after the appearance of this advertisement. No mention of the works can be found in any of the trade journals after 1903. Thus, it is likely that actual production of "Gibson Girl" was limited. Very few shapes are known, and even these are seldom seen today. The Keystone Tumbler Works primarily manufactured tumblers and bar goods. Perhaps National Glass shut down production at this factory in one of their many economy cutbacks, and concentrated Keystone's specialty in the nearby Rochester Tumbler Company.

Kamm reports that "Gibson Girl" is known in a 4-piece table set (creamer, sugar, spooner, butter), a tumbler and a 10½" plate. Metz had nothing to add to this unusually limited list. It would be interesting to learn of the existence of other pieces. This researcher would appreciate hearing from collectors for future validation of any unlisted items in this pattern. Write me at Box 102, Jonesville, Mich. 49250.

Reprint of full-page advertisement (Dec., 1903) announcing
the pattern known today as "Gibson Girl" (upper right).

"GONTERMAN SWIRL"—A TESTAMENT TO GLASS CREATIVENESS

This week I will be offering my findings on a pattern of such unique charm and beauty that it seems almost unbelievable it has been virtually ignored in existing books on pattern identification. As a result, it has become known by so many names as to create confusion among collectors and minimize collectibility. It is frequently referred to as "Ribbed Swirl" (a name confused with other patterns), "Francis Ware Swirl" (a totally different line), and as "Gonterman." This last name also belongs to another pattern (Metz II, plate 2097), but the two have so many similar pattern characteristics, I have named the illustrated pattern "Gonterman Swirl" in my book to retain a combination of the names by which it is already known.

The true "Gonterman" has beads and ribs vertically embossed around the pattern, with an amber-*stained* top rim. The "Gonterman Swirl" pattern has parallel beads and ribs on the base of most pieces, and the top is true colored glass—*not stained*. Both can be found with the lower portion of the pattern frosted. However, our featured pattern was made with either an amber or a blue top, and also with an opalescent base. The upper portion of the pattern is a separate piece of colored glass which is annealed to the base portion while the glass is still hot.

Certain pieces of "Gonterman Swirl" are frequently found with the patent date August 5, 1876, embossed under the rim of the base. This has convinced a number of glass collectors that this is a rare form of Centennial Glass. It most certainly is not! This pattern is strictly Victorian in concept, and toothpick holders in pattern glass didn't make their appearance until the next decade. It is my contention that the date refers to a patent acquired by Louis Wagner in August, 1876, patenting a process whereby two separately formed pieces of glass are joined to form a single item. This patent was originally used for stemware and apparently revived for this pattern at a later date.

Mr. Wagner was associated with Hobbs, Brockunier & Company of Wheeling, W.Va., at this time, and it is to this manufacturer that I attribute *both* "Gonterman" patterns. In 1886, reports started appearing in trade journals stating that the demand for Hobbs, Brockunier's "Pineapple Set" had exceeded their anticipations. Later that year, the same set was advertised by Hobbs as "Pressed Opalescent, Patented." Unfortunately, no illustrations accompanied the ad. No patents exist for any pattern resembling a pineapple, so it is likely that "Gonterman Swirl" is the pattern which was advertised and the annealing process is the patent referred to. With a little imagination— something the Hobbs glassmakers had no shortage of—this pattern somewhat resembles a squatty little pineapple (a characteristic especially apparent on the sugar bowl).

Despite its known popularity, Hobb's production of "Gonterman Swirl" was obviously limited, as pieces are very hard to find today. The annealing process undoubtedly proved costly in manpower, and sales were just as good on the Francis Ware lines which were cheaper to produce. Also, this annealing process was not always successful as some pieces can be found with obvious production flaws, (bent, lopsided, misaligned, etc.)

"Gonterman Swirl" can still be found today at relatively bargain prices considering its proud origins and rarity. The blue top pieces are definitely more scarce today than the amber. Also, the opalescent-base pieces are rarer than the frosted. The pattern was made in a complete table service, including a rare cruet and syrup jug. Also known (Fig. B) is a gas shade (ever consider a collection of pattern glass shades? — a good number were made).

A few pieces of this beautiful "Gonterman Swirl" pattern are on exhibit at the Oglebay Institute at Wheeling, W.Va. This is an outstanding museum which I highly recommend to any student of early American glass. The Institute also attributes this pattern to Hobbs, Brockunier & Company.

FIGURE B—(l. to r.) Opal. Base-Amber top toothpick, (note pineapple shape); Blue top-Frosted base toothpick in original silver-plate frame; Blue top-Frosted base cruet, original-stopper (note the unique handle also found on the creamer & syrup); Blue top-opal. base gas shade.

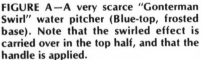

FIGURE A—A very scarce "Gonterman Swirl" water pitcher (Blue-top, frosted base). Note that the swirled effect is carried over in the top half, and that the handle is applied.

"GRAPEVINE AND CHERRY SPRIG"
Another of those unlisted Northwood Patterns

Again I am presenting information on a Northwood pattern not yet documented in existing glass literature. I have named the pattern *Grapevine and Cherry Sprig* since the name "Grape and Cherry" has already been assigned to a novelty bowl made in carnival and opalescent glass. This week's featured line was made only in crystal, so there should be little confusion concerning the two patterns.

Illustrated here is a large master berry bowl and the small individual bowl which accompanies it as part of a berry set. *Grapevine and Cherry Sprig* was also made in a four-piece table setting (covered butter, creamer, covered sugar and spoon holder), and a water set. Most pieces are footed, except for the tumblers. All pieces seen by this writer have been marked with the distinctive "N-in-a-Circle" trademark of Harry Northwood & Company, of Wheeling, W.Va. The trademark dates after 1905, and we can assume this pattern dates shortly afterward.

The pattern usually is gold decorated at the upper rim, and is reported with frosted glass fruit. It probably was also made with color-stained fruit, a common practice among glass factories around 1905-1910. A few examples may even exist in colored glass or carnival glass, but these should be classified as extreme rarities.

After 1905, most glass factories severely limited the number of items available in a tableware pattern. I have never seen or heard of a salt shaker, toothpick holder, goblet, cruet or syrup in *Grapevine and Cherry Sprig,* but that does not mean they don't exist. Indeed, if they do I would most definitely be interested in hearing about them. Their existence will be documented in a later column in this series. Write me at Box 28087, Columbus, Ohio 43228.

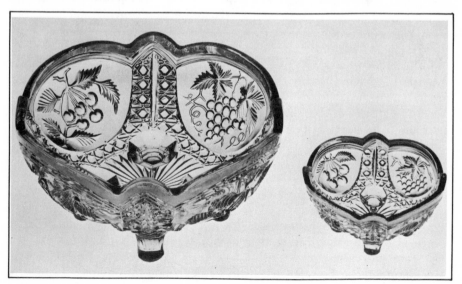

WILL THE REAL "HENRIETTA" PATTERN PLEASE STAND UP?

With this week's column, I hope to clear up some long-standing confusion concerning two very similar patterns which have inadvertantly become known by the same name. Normally this would not be considered terribly unique. Quite a few different patterns carry identical names. There are several *Columbias, Victorias, Priscillas,* as well as two very popular patterns known as *Amberette.* However, these names were original manufacturers' names, and the fault does not lie with our glass historians.

And yet a case in point where confusion *has* been created by an inaccurate listing is the *Henrietta* pattern. Figure A is a reprint from a U.S. Glass Company 1891 catalogue, which shows the Number 335 pattern of their Factory "H" (Hobbs Glass Company, Wheeling, W.Va.). Unfortunately, this pattern was listed as *Henrietta* in a popular 1968 publication covering ruby-stained glass. Despite the surface similarity, Hobbs' #335 is *not* Henrietta at all. This line is not to be found in Kamm, Metz or Lee, but the salt shaker *is* included in Peterson's book on that subject, and he provided the name *Hexagon Block.* I feel this name should hereafter be retained when identifying Hobbs' #335. This attractive pattern was made in crystal, etched amber-stained and ruby-stained (rarely etched).

Figure B is a reprint from another 1891 U.S. Glass catalogue illustrating the *real Henrietta* pattern, and it should be easy to note the differences in the two patterns when they are seen side-by-side as shown here. Production was carried on at their Factory "C", the Columbia Glass Company at Findlay, Ohio. The true *Henrietta* pattern was made primarily in crystal, and is very rare in ruby-stained.

The catalogues in which I was fortunate to find these reprints were through the courtesy of the Carnegie Institute, where a wealth of original U.S. Glass catalogues were available for study. The undocumented data which I found in these catalogues is staggering, and I am extremely grateful to this institute and its staff for their cooperation with my research.

Henrietta is much more rare than *Hexagon Block,* and several unfortunate Findlay glass collectors have responded to ads listing the Figure A pattern as *Henrietta,* only to have their hopes dashed when the package arrived.

Adding more fuel to this pattern confusion, the ever-popular *Red Block* is strikingly similar to both patterns shown here, as it also carries hexagons as a primary pattern motif.

The simplest way to tell them apart? *Red Block* is just that—the blocks are stained red. *Hexagon Block* is found ruby-stained only at the top, with the blocks left clear. And finally, *Henrietta* is so rare in ruby-stained that I cannot personally vouch for its existence (Metz claims it was made). I, therefore, cannot be certain where the color-staining would be located. However, the unique difference in this pattern is the combination of "fat" and "thin" hexagons.

Kamm states that *Henrietta* was earlier made by Adams & Company, circa 1874. Perhaps the molds were transferred to the Findlay plant after both Adams and Columbia became part of the giant U.S. Glass combine.

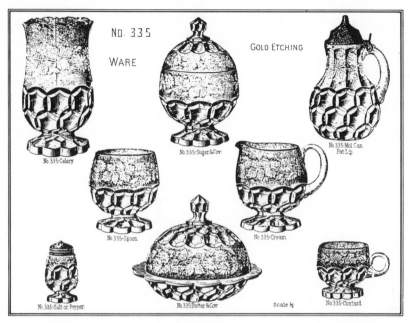

FIGURE A—Catalogue reprint from 1891 U.S. Glass catalogue, showing an assortment of "Hexagon Block" pattern (Factory "H"—Hobbs Glass Co.). This pattern is often mistaken for "Henrietta."

FIGURE B—Catalogue reprint from 1891 U.S. Glass Catalogue, showing an assortment of "Henrietta" pattern (Factory "C"—Columbia Glass Co.).

"HOBNAIL WITH PANELLED THUMBPRINT"

To the best of my knowledge, this week's featured pattern is listed for the first time ever in this column. I have carefully scanned the pages of Kamm, Metz and Lee, and nowhere does it appear.

The Hobnail motif was very popular for tableware from as early as 1880 and production in one form or another has continued to this very day. Due to this popularity, as many as a dozen different companies made their own version of this glass. Slight differences in mold design were undertaken to avoid legal repercussions.

At first glance, the table set illustrated appears to be the *Hobnail with Thumbprint* pattern which was made by Doyle & Company around 1885. However, it most decidedly is not. The thumbprints at the base of this pattern are raised up somewhat, and each one is framed inside separate panels. *Hobnail with Thumbprint* was never made in opalescent glass, and the table set illustrated is in a deep, lovely shade of canary yellow opalescent.

Since this pattern has not been officially listed and named, I have dubbed it "Hobnail with Panelled Thumbprint" in my recent publication on opalescent pattern glass. All pieces, except for the butter dish, have the thumbprints at the base of the pattern.

This pattern has only been seen by this researcher in opalescent colors of blue and canary. However, it is likely that it was also produced in white opalescent, as well as plain crystal.

I am not positive who made *Hobnail with Panelled Thumbprint,* but it is interesting that all pieces to this set have a well defined circle on the inside base. Many sources credit this circular marking, even without the famous "N" inside it, to Northwood, although I cannot personally confirm this speculation. However, I definitely feel that this pattern was made around 1905, and this decidedly limits the possibilities.

Production of this pattern was undoubtedly limited, as it is not easily found today. Only the table set and berry set have been reported to date, but a water set most likely was also made. No toothpick holder, salt shakers or cruet is known, a certain sign of later production. After 1904, the glass factories were considerably limiting the number of items offered in each pattern they introduced. This was a necessary economic cutback in order for them to survive during highly competitive times. This explains why the popular carnival glass, produced after 1906, was seldom made in toothpicks, salt shakers, cruets, and other items which were frequently made a mere ten years before.

Hobnail with Panelled Thumbprint is not as collectible as some of the other variations of Hobnail. This is due to the fact that it remained unlisted until now, and collectors fear what they are not familiar with. The most popular Hobnail is that which was mass produced by the brilliant craftsmen at Hobbs, Brockunier & Co., Wheeling, W.Va. Their version was a line of mold-brown ware, and is not considered pattern glass at all by most discriminating collectors. Hobbs' Hobnail is especially collectible in the popular *Frances Ware* decoration.

It is interesting to note that if indeed Northwood did manufacture *Hobnail with Panelled Thumbprint,* it would have been produced in the same factory as the Hobbs version. Harry Northwood worked at Hobbs at the time of their Hobnail production, and in 1902 purchased and re-opened the long-idle plant in which he worked almost twenty years prior. He was undoubtedly influenced by the production undertaken at Hobbs during his early career.

"Hobnail with Panelled Thumbprint" 4-piece table set. Note that the butter dish lacks the thumbprints which distinguishes this pattern from the many other Hobnail-type patterns.

"INSIDE RIBBING"
An Example of Double-Name Confusion

It isn't often that a glass researcher such as myself has such a perfect opportunity to offer updated data and to correct information of earlier authorities. This series even makes it possible for me to correct my own mistakes, without waiting (and hoping) for my books to go into a second, updated, printing. Most authors continue to print their works without change, mistakes and all, which represents a gross misjustice to their readers. The whole purpose of research is to present the truth to the best of our ability, and to those handful of writers who believe in these same standards, I am sure I join thousands of others in saluting you.

This week, I humbly bow to the earlier listing of a pattern which I had previously thought to be listed for the first time in my book. A few devoted readers called this to my attention, and I thank them. The pattern was named "Inside Ribbing" by Mrs. Kamm (Book 8, pg. 37), and is illustrated here in a reprint of a full page ad which I found in a December, 1900, issue of "Illustrated Glass & Pottery World."

It is unfortunate that this oversight in the Kamm listing was discovered after publication of my book, as I named the pattern "Pressed Optic." I sincerely regret this oversight, as I am now responsible for a single pattern being known by two different names. This is a practice which collectors have condemned for years, and the responsibility rests on the "authorities" who were either too lazy or too pompous to honor the previously published listings of their colleagues.

This same condemnation can be applied to those researchers who have named "their" patterns with names which were earlier used on a completely different pattern. I won't go into specifics here, but in some cases as many as three different patterns carry the same name. In one unique case, a glass writer named one pattern in one book, then used the same exact name for a different pattern in another. This practice must be controlled for future generations of collectors who will look to these pioneering publications for answers—not further confusion.

As for my own inadvertant contribution to this confusion, I will be correcting this and all other mistakes in my own publications as they go into second printings. "Inside Ribbing" is a lovely pattern (especially in color) which should become quite popular in the future, and I do not want it to be known by more than one name.

Our featured pattern was made in crystal, and in colors of vaseline, emerald green, and also ruby-stained. This last color was a solid color coating on the glass exterior, and I have only seen souvenir toothpick holders in this color to date. "Inside Ribbing" also had very limited production in opalescent colors of vaseline, green and possibly blue. It is rare in this color, and most appealing—especially with enamel decoration.

The illustrated ad by W. E. Cummings & Co., a manufacturer's jobber from Chicago, does not name who actually made this pattern. Neither does Kamm. Further research turned up an early Beaumont Glass Company ad which identified this as their No. 101 line, with their No. 74 decoration. I found this ad most unusual, as this Martins Ferry, Ohio firm was a member of the National Glass Company, at this time and it was unique for one of the member factories to undertake independent advertising.

Beaumont Glass Co., run by Harry Northwood's brother-in-law, relocated to Grafton, W.Va. around 1905. Before the year was over, the plant ceased operation for a number of reasons.

"Inside Ribbing" was made in a complete table service. Besides the water set, berry set and table set, there is a cruet set (cruet, salt & pepper on matching tray), celery vase, syrup jug, toothpick holder and jelly compote. The pattern is fortunately not plagued by reproductions.

W. E. CUMMINGS & CO.

Nothing Sells Better for the Holidays

THAN FANCY

DECORATED GLASS

This shows a few pieces in our No. 101 Optic line. Made in Crystal or Canary and decorated in Enamel colors. It is Rich, attractive and salable. Write us for more complete list.

We show the greatest line in Chicago, the product of seven factories

4-Piece Condiment Sets.
Crystal Decorated ..... $4.50 doz. sets
Canary Decorated ..... 5.25 doz. sets

We have many other styles we would like to show you Rose, Ruby and Opal, as well as all the opalescent colors, either plain or decorated.

Crystal Decorated
Canary Decorated

7-Piece Berry Sets.
Crystal, Green, Blue, Canary, Amber.
$6.50 Per doz.
7.00 Per doz.

If

you have never handled

Sea Shells

...and...

Shell Novelties

You are missing the brightest, most showy and best selling line of Specialties possible for holiday trade. Our "Hustlers' Helps" will tell you more about the line. Send us your orders for

Crockery, Glassware, Lamps, Shells, Novelties and Souvenirs.

We Represent Manufacturers in These Lines and Can Place Your Orders to Advantage.

Address...

4-Piece Sets.
Crystal Decorated $5.00 doz.
Canary Decorated $5.50 doz.

W. E. CUMMINGS & CO.

160 State St., Cor. Monroe, Chicago.

An early ad of W. E. Cummings & Co. showing some "Inside Ribbing" pieces.

"THE JEFFERSON OPTIC PATTERN"

Little did I know when my first book was published that included among its pages was a pattern which was destined to become quite popular. Using toothpick holders for identification I named this week's featured pattern "Tiny Optic." I chose this name because I was unaware at the time that this little toothpick actually was a small part of a matching table-setting.

Needless to say, the use of the word "tiny" in identifying larger pieces to this set would be inappropriate. As Volume 4 of my series (Custard Glass from A to Z) goes to press I'm officially re-naming this pattern to include the manufacturer's name. Hereafter, the pieces shown here should be referred to as *Jefferson Optic.*

The pattern is illustrated here in a rare rose-decorated toothpick and salt & pepper. Usually these items are found with souvenir labeling. It was one of these souvenir toothpicks which revealed to me the actual maker of the pattern. This toothpick was marked "Krys-tol", a trademark used by the Jefferson Glass Company of Follansbee, W.Va. after 1913. However few of the rose-decorated pieces have been found trademarked, which makes me believe they date around 1908.

The pattern earlier was named simply "Rose" by Brahmer in her publication on custard glass. However this name is now known to be inappropriate because the same identical pieces have been seen with other forms of enamel decoration or the previously mentioned souvenir stenciling.

Jefferson Optic was made in colors other than the custard shown here. It is also available in a rich shade of amethyst, cobalt blue, emerald green and vaseline. Items made include the 4-piece table-set, the water set, berry set, cruet set (a cruet and salt/pepper on a cloverleaf tray), toothpick and finger bowl (seen only as souvenir ware).

The Optic name is derived from the ribbed effect seen inside the glass when held up to a strong light. Most, but not all, pieces of *Jefferson Optic* have this characteristic.

In custard glass this little-known pattern will some day be quite sought after due to its extreme rarity in this color. In fact, *Jefferson Optic* (without souveniring) is one of the hardest patterns in which to complete a set. This rarity deserves special attention among collectors.

Scarce Rose-decorated Jefferson Optic salt/pepper and toothpick holder in custard glass. The shakers have pink roses, the toothpick has red roses.

"JEWEL & FESTOON"

To date, this column has devoted its attention to the finer forms of pattern glass—the blown opalescent, the custard, the cased opaque, and the satin glass. This type of glass seldom comes to mind when one thinks of "Pattern glass." And yet it most certainly is. They are designed with a pattern which comprises a complete set. Sometimes a "set" is nothing more than a seasoning service (salt, pepper, mustard, syrup, sugar shaker, & possibly toothpick). But they are all distinctly different items of mutual design, and thus should be termed "pattern glass." Yet thousands of people still think of pattern glass as pressed crystal, completely devoid of color.

Indeed, this week's featured pattern was made primarily in clear glass, but some pieces were produced in milk glass. Kamm first called it "Jewel & Festoon", but it is also known as "Loop & Jewel" (Lee) and is often affectionately referred to as "Queen's Necklace." It is a simple but pleasing pattern, which is very impressive in a table service.

None of the earlier glass authorities seemed to know who made this pattern. Mrs. Metz reported that it was made in Ohio in the late 1880s. Mrs. Lee also dated the glass from the 1880s. However, they were both wrong on both counts. The pattern was made in Indiana, and was introduced in late 1903.

Illustrated is a December, 1903 advertisement which I found in an issue of "Glass & Pottery World", an early industry trade journal. It reveals that the pattern was introduced by the National Glass Company, and actual production taking place at the Beatty-Brady Glass Works of Dunkirk, Indiana. Thus we witness a pattern of such superior design and glass quality, that even the experts thought it was of earlier vintage.

After the failure of the National Glass Company (circa 1906), the factory became the Indiana Glass Company, and "Jewel & Festoon" continued to be produced by its new maker; thus some production could date as late as 1915. Not exactly as early as this pattern's collectors had hoped, I'm certain.

Originally called the "Venus" pattern by its makers, it is available only in a limited number of pieces. Mrs. Lee mentions that she had not witnessed a goblet prior to publication of her book, and indeed the simple reason was that goblets were not in vogue after 1900. This is an important factor in dating pattern glass—was a goblet made? If a toothpick was made in a pattern, it would likely date between 1890 and 1905. Anything before or after those dates generally lacked a matching toothpick holder to the set. The pieces which *were* made in "Jewel & Festoon" are a table set (creamer, sugar, butter, spooner), a syrup jug, an 8", 7" and 6" bowl, a 4" sauce, an 8" pickle dish, a 6½" comport, and a 5" square dish. Dr. Peterson shows a milk glass salt shaker in his book, but this item is not illustrated in the early catalogues. Mrs. Lee also lists a water pitcher, sherbert cups, and a footed salt. This large salt actually is the open sugar to a "tankard" shaped individual creamer.

A portion of the December, 1903 ad which introduced the "Venus" pattern, better known today as "Jewel & Festoon."

"KLEAR-KUT"

Illustrated here is a ruby-stained water pitcher which does not appear in the pattern glass books of Kamm, Lee, Metz or even Heacock. In fact, it doesn't even appear in Barrett's book on ruby-stained pattern glass. So what is it?

Most glass collectors don't own the 100 books or more it would take to have a complete reference library—and that would just cover pattern glass. It wouldn't include Art Glass or Depression Glass or Sandwich Glass. But if you happen to have a copy of the Miller's book on the early years of the New Martinsville Glass Company, you would find this water pitcher's pattern shown in a table set, appropriately named KLEAR-KUT by the Millers.

The New Martinsville Glass Company made a late entry into the pattern glass field, so their lines of tableware were limited to a select number, both plain and ornate. Most of their patterned tableware was in clear glass, but some of their lines lent themselves well to ruby-staining. Other patterns made by this firm which are known in ruby-stain are Carnation, Horseshoe Medallion, Heart and Sand (very rare and quite valuable), Lorraine and Placid Thumbprint. Very little actual colored pattern glass was made by this company.

KLEAR-KUT was made in a water set, table set and berry set. No toothpick holder, salt shaker or cruet have been reported to date.

89

"LADDER WITH DIAMOND"
Is it Duncan or Tarentum Glass?

This week I will attempt to clear up some confusion which has prevailed over two almost identical patterns known as "Ladder with Diamond." The pattern name was initiated by Kamm in her eighth book, but she was unable to identify by whom this line was made.

Dr. Peterson (in his salt shaker book) did list the Tarentum Glass Company, of Tarentum, Pa. as its maker, but unfortunately illustrated a second, very similar shaker—also calling it *Ladder with Diamond*. The patterns are so much alike that for them both to carry the same name creates additional confusion. Peterson correctly attributed the twin pattern to Duncan & Miller (Washington, Pa.), in 1904, but apparently had no record of the company's number for this new line, Number 52. Thus I believe this Duncan version of the pattern should be referred to as "D & M #52" in the future to avoid confusion with the Tarentum variant.

Illustrated in Figures A-C are a number of items reprinted from a 1903 trade journal featuring in detail a number of pieces in Tarentum's *Ladder with Diamond*. Note the slight difference in the creamer shown in Figure A and the one shown in Figure C. Perhaps one is the creamer to the table setting and the other an individual or breakfast size creamer. Also notice the "Cheese Dish" in Figure B, a relatively scarce item in pattern glass.

Due to the large variety of pieces made in this Tarentum line, and the differences in the pattern design to accommodate individual pieces, there is only one sure way to tell the Tarentum and Duncan patterns apart. On the Tarentum version, the "diamonds" are filled with tiny hexagonal (six-sided) buttons. On the Duncan line, the "diamonds" are filled with other tiny diamonds. There are other noticeable differences, but the simplest rule of thumb is that Tarentum used buttons—Duncan used diamonds.

Both patterns were made primarily in crystal, but the Tarentum pattern was also released in a line of ruby-stained ware, very rarely found today. Perhaps the Duncan version was also made in a line of color-stained glass, but I cannot confirm this at the present time.

Note the finger bowl in the Figure D grouping, which reveals for the first time the numbered identification. Duncan & Miller are already well known for their #42 pattern, which today is highly collectible.

I should note here that both the D & M #42 and the D & M #52 patterns were reproduced in the 1950's in a crystal punch set (a large two-piece bowl, cups and underplate).

TARENTUM GLASS COMPANY

...... TARENTUM, PA. ......

MANUFACTURERS OF PRESSED GLASSWARE

NEW YORK OFFICE: 24 PARK PLACE. ═══════════ D. R. MARSHALL

FIGURE A—Reprint from a 1903 trade journal featuring the "latest" line of pressed glassware made by Tarentum, known today as "Ladder with Diamond."

FIGURE B—Reprint from 1903 journal, illustrating a Ladder with Diamond water pitcher and cheese dish.

CHEESE DISH.

PITCHER.

FIGURE C—Another Ladder with Diamond creamer with slightly different pattern characteristics than the one shown in Figure A.

NO. 52. FINGER BOWL. DUNCAN & MILLER GLASS CO.

DUNCAN & MILLER GLASS CO. NEW HOTEL SUGAR.

DUNCAN & MILLER GLASS CO. NEW HOTEL CREAM.

FIGURE D—1904 Grouping of "Duncan & Miller #52" pieces, often confused for the similar Tarentum pattern.

"LEAF MOLD" —
The Long-neglected "Sleeper"

This week I will be offering my findings on a pattern which has heretofore been virtually ignored in existing books on pattern identification. "Leaf Mold" is the name most often used today, listed in Taylor's book on sugar shakers. It has also been labeled "Leaf Spears" (Boultinghouse, plt. 145) and "Rose" (Peterson's "Salt Shakers," pg. 37-T), but these names are seldom used in this pattern's identification. I have also heard it referred to as "Artichoke" and "Cabbage Rose," but these names only cause confusion with similarly named patterns.

Considerable research was undertaken in an attempt to correctly report the origins of this pattern in my book. This was no easy task, as early ads for "Leaf Mold" have not been reported previously, or turned up through my own efforts. Thus glass, color and pattern characteristics are important in attributing its maker, and this pattern was produced in no less than a dozen different colors and finishes. So attribution in this case should be considered nothing more than an educated theory.

"Leaf Mold" has definite characteristics of both the Northwood Glass Company *and* Hobbs, Brockunier & Co., both from the Wheeling, W.Va. area. It should be noted here that Mr. Northwood worked for Hobbs early in his career, and was no doubt influenced by (or influential in) the exciting production undertaken by Hobbs in the early 1880s. The possibility exists that this pattern was originally made by Hobbs, Brockunier, during its later years, circa 1890, just prior to their merger with and subsequent closing by the U.S. Glass Company. The molds for "Leaf Mold" were probably purchased by Northwood after the 1892 shutdown, and he produced several lines in his own colors. Such practices were common at this time—Beaumont Glass (established by Northwood's brother-in-law in a vacated Northwood factory) reissued dozens of old Hobbs' molds around 1896.

A major reason for the Northwood attribution can be seen in the accompanying illustration (Fig. A) which reveals that the finial of the Northwood Royal Ivy cased-spatter butter and sugar is exactly the same as the one found on the "Leaf Mold" pieces. This bud-like finial, however, is not found on the crystal and rubina Royal Ivy pieces, as they were introduced in 1889, three years before the Hobbs shutdown.

"Leaf Mold" was probably first made by Hobbs in a beautiful cased glass, combining splashes of cranberry color with tiny flakes of mica. This "Vasa Murrhina" process was patented by William Leighton, Jr., in 1883, employed by Hobbs at the time. Also produced were opaque colors of white, blue, turquoise green and possibly pink. These colors (and the "Leaf Mold" pattern design) are characteristic of the creations of Nicholas Kopp, Jr., a mold designer and color genius who worked for Hobbs, Brockunier prior to the closing. Mr. Kopp, long ignored by glass historians despite his major contributions for many years, later was responsible for the production of similar opaque patterns (Florette, Guttate, Cone, etc.) as manager of the factories of the Consolidated Lamp & Glass Co. The last Hobbs color, and by far the rarest, is a rubina line (cranberry to clear) with opalescent swirls in the glass. This color was undoubtedly experimental, with actual production limited.

After the proposed Northwood acquisition of the molds, this pattern was made in a vaseline glass with spatterings of cranberry and white color, in both glossy and frosted finish. The craquelle line of Royal Ivy is in a very similar color, also found in dual finishes. Northwood also produced "Leaf Mold" in satin glass colors of crystal (camphor), blue, vaseline and cranberry. Northwood's "Parian Swirl" (my book, Figures 228 & 229) can be found in strikingly similar colors.

It is possible, indeed likely, that all colors of "Leaf Mold" were made by Northwood. However, with glass characteristics as our only clue to attribution, dual credit seems the most likely answer at this time.

With so many colors available, "Leaf Mold" is a sheer delight to collect. Pieces are seldom seen in shops and antiques shows, so the challenge of the "search" adds to its desirability. Since so little information regarding it has been offered to date, this pattern can still be found at reasonable—even "sleeper" prices. "Leaf Mold" was made in a full range of table pieces, and novelty items like rose bowls and perfumes. Why not start your collection right away, before prices skyrocket on this exciting pattern with such proud origins.

Leaf Mold toothpick holder.

FIGURE A—Finial on Royal Ivy cased-spatter butter—the same one found on the Leaf Mold butter.

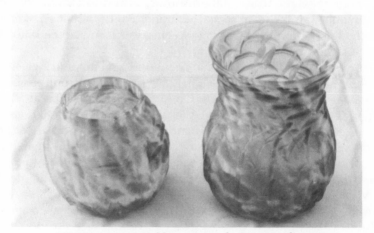

FIGURE B—Leaf Mold spooner and very rare celery vase.

94

FIGURE C—Rare Leaf Mold pickle caster in cranberry satin, a color which matches Northwoods Parian Swirl (shown here in a butter-note finial).

"MCKINLEY BY MCKEE"

Illustrated here is a reprint from an 1896 "China, Glass & Lamps" which features three items in political glassware featuring the profile of presidential candidate William McKinley. This advertisement appeared just prior to the elections, so McKee must have been fairly confident of the outcome for them to have purchased a full-page ad.

Other commemorative items not shown in the ad, but mentioned at the bottom, include a tumbler with McKinley's head pressed in the bottom, and a blown tumbler with etched profiles of McKinley and his running mate, Garrat Hobart.

The plate and tumblers are listed in Lindsay's book on American historical glass, but she does not mention the mug, which no doubt is quite rare. These items are all known only in clear glass, and crystal with gold, with the latter more desirable.

The figure of William McKinley appears on several other glass novelties, probably more than any other presidential figure, excluding perhaps George Washington. Certainly this was because his presidency was at a time when the glass industry was at its peak. Also his assassination in 1901 resulted in a wave of public desire four souvenirs commemorating their lost President, and the glass industry was more than willing to meet this demand.

Other McKinley items include a rectangular tray with McKinley holding an open scroll (rare), an oval memorial tray with McKinley holding a closed scroll (more common), several different round plates in all sizes (clear or milk glass), a small cup plate with a transfer portrait, a covered mug in crystal, several tumblers and a frosted glass statuette. No doubt there are others.

McKinley was a Republican candidate in 1896, running against William Jennings Bryan, and the term "Protection and Plenty" shown in this featured ad was the party's campaign slogan.

McKee & Brothers joined the ill-fated National Glass Company merger in 1899, and later moved to their present location at Jeanette, Pennsylvania.

96

MELONETTE—AN UNLISTED KOPP CREATION

Most collectors of fine Victorian colored glassware are familiar with the brilliance and beauty of the cased glass patterns *Florette, Guttate and Cone.* Earlier this series dealt with the equally lovely *Bulging Loops.* All of these patterns were testaments to the genius of Nicholas Kopp, who shared his talents as a glass chemist with both the Consolidated Lamp & Glass Co., and the Pittsburgh Lamp, Brass & Glass Co., from 1894 to as late as 1910. Previously, he received much of his background training while working for the Hobbs Glass Co., at Wheeling, W.Va., and later he opened his own company in Pennsylvania which is still operating today (making glass for stop lights primarily).

Listed here is a pattern which has to date escaped the attention of glass researchers, including myself. The water pitcher shown is in a deep and lovely pink opaque with an outer casing of crystal. The tumbler is in a lovely shade of cranberry.* There is no doubt in my mind whatsoever that these pieces were designed and produced by Mr. Kopp, circa 1895, while he was associated with Consolidated (their factory was located at Fostoria, Ohio at this time, but shortly afterward the plant relocated to Coraopolis, Pa.).

Since the pattern is unlisted, I am officially naming her "Melonette." Information concerning this pattern is somewhat sketchy at this time. To date I have only witnessed the two pieces shown here and a tiny blubous salt shaker (in pink opaque—not cased). Other items are likely, but I do not wish to speculate on their existence at this time. As they turn up or are reported to me (with documentative photos), I will report them in a later column in this series.

Care should be taken not to confuse *Melonette* with other similarly designed .melon-ribbed patterns. These others are found primarily in salt shakers & sugar shakers (Little Shrimp,) with no known water set.

Nicholas Kopp was a genius in color experimentation. It never ceases to amaze me as an unlisted color turns up around every corner. Thus, it would be impossible for me to pinpoint the colors in which *Melonette* can be found, but a sampling of possible colors would include the following:
   1. Opaque white, pink, pale green, turquoise blue, pale blue
   2. Cased (outer layer of crystal) pink, yellow, green & blue
   3. Crystal, cranberry, pigeon blood red, red satin
   4. Satin finish pink, white, yellow, blue, green, and a very rare apricot

If the above listing of colors is not enough to convince you of the creative genius of the long-overlooked Nicholas Kopp, Jr., then nothing will.

I now know that this tumbler is not the one designed for the Melonette pitcher. A picture of this set in blue cased was sent to me and the tumblers were different.

"MEDALLION SPRIG"

Not much is known about the West Virginia Glass Company or their actual production, but our featured pattern attests to the fact that they employed some of the finest glassmakers available. The name most often used for this pattern is "Medallion Sprig" (courtesy of Dr. Peterson). It has also been labelled "Stylistic Leaf" (Boultinghouse), but this name is seldom used today.

This pattern is not listed in Kamm, Metz or Lee—however a close look in Kamm 6, plate 4, reveals a lemonade set in an 1895 Montgomery Wards catalog reprint. She calls it an "Unnamed, pressed glass set." On the contrary, "Medallion Sprig" is not pressed at all. It is a mold-blown ware, made in a wide range of colors, many of which are not found in any other pattern. These totally unique colors intrigued me for quite some time. I spent hours searching through old journals and pattern glass reference books, hoping to find some clue as to who was responsible for this exciting-pattern. The pattern and color characteristics leaned strongly towards Hobbs, Brockunier & Company of Wheeling, W.Va., as its maker. However, the 1895 Wards ad mentioned above overruled this possibility since Hobbs was taken over and closed down by the big U.S. Glass Company three years before.

During a second check of these old glass journals, I spotted an ad which I missed in my first search. I was delighted to "re-discover" this long forgotten advertisement, and I have reprinted it here (Figure A) for your enjoyment. Perhaps the reason I missed it during the earlier research was because the pattern design is somewhat squatty in the 8" bowl illustrated. Thus, I have included a line drawing (Figure B) of the toothpick holder which reveals the "Medallion Sprig" pattern characteristics to better advantage.

The Hobbs' characteristics can be easily explained. Martin's Ferry, Ohio is just across the river from Wheeling, W.Va. With the closing of the big Hobbs' plant, many of the designers and craftsmen relocated with the factories in production at nearby Martin's Ferry—among them the Northwood, Buckeye, Beaumont and West Virginia Glass companies. In fact, one of the heads of WVG was Hanson E. Waddell, who was in fact earlier associated with Hobbs, Brockunier. Perhaps this association was directly responsible for the extreme similarities in the production of the two companies.

What distinguishes "Medallion Sprig" from other patterns is the totally unique colors in which the pattern is found. Primary production, listed in the Figure A advertisement, was in light "tints" of blue, green, violet and ruby (today referred to as cranberry), all graduating to clear at the base of the pattern. Thus, the cranberry shade is quite collectible as "rubina" glass. However, the other three shades are unlike any others in pattern glass—with rare Northwood exceptions.

As if these lovely colors were not enough, the pattern can also be found in all clear crystal solid amber (rare) and milk glass. "Medallion Sprig" was made in a complete table service, at least 14 different shapes. The butter dish is particularly exciting. However, the base is all clear, with the color tint appearing only in the bottom half of the dome lid.

This color "tint" is not a painted or a dipped "wash" of color staining. It is actually color "flashed" with a thin coating of colored glass, similar to the process used on the rubina verde (cranberry to green) glass. This is quality glassware at its finest, and should not be classified as color-stained.

This color process must have proved costly—however the water set, with metal tray, originally sold for only $1.35. Today the pattern is seldom found in shops or antiques shows, and in many forms "Medallion Sprig" is very rare. Especially scarce is the butter dish and water pitcher, perhaps because the pieces are extremely lightweight for their size, and highly susceptible to damage.

West Virginia Glass Company closed down in 1896 due to poor business, but was reopened for a short time when the National Glass Company absorbed the factory in 1899. Other patterns which can be attributed to this fine glass company are "Scroll with Cane Band", "I.O.U.", and the No. 203 blown "Optic" line, also available in several opalescent variants, including "Fern" and "Daisy & Fern". None of their patterns have ever been reproduced.

West Virginia Glass Co.,
MARTIN'S FERRY, OHIO.

We make a large line of 209 Blown Ware in 4 TINTED COLORS.
Blue Tint, Emerald Tint, Violet Tint, and Ruby Tint.
The finest line of Glassware ever put on the market.
Cuts furnished on application.

8 in. 209 Blown Bowl, with Shoulder
FOR SILVER PLATERS.

FIGURE A—This advertisement was found in an 1894 issue of "China, Glass and Lamps", an early industry trade journal.

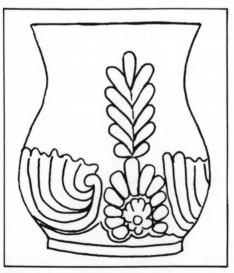

FIGURE B—"Medallion Sprig" toothpick holder.

THE "NESTOR" PATTERN

It seems that around every corner there are new discoveries to be found through glass research, which makes this study one of the most exciting and rewarding for any lover of antique glassware. This week I will be attributing a rather popular pattern with nothing more than design, color and decoration techniques as clues. I have uncovered no early ads or catalogues listing this pattern, so I am going out on a limb, somewhat, reporting these findings.

Illustrated in Figure A is a grouping of pieces in this week's featured pattern, which was originally called *Nestor* in a 1903 Montgomery Wards catalogue. The pattern can be found with or without a delicate enamel decoration with gliding. Figure B is a sketch of this intricate decoration which frequently graces this pattern.

I wish you could see this set in color. The cruet set to the right (and the toothpick) are in a lovely shade of amethyst. The cruet on the left is a deep electric blue, and barely visible is the decoration. *Nestor* was also made in apple green.

Close inspection of the tray to the cruet set will reveal something rather startling. This tray is in the pattern known as "Chrysanthemum Sprig", which to date has only been reported in the popular blue and ivory shades of custard glass. This illustrated tray is in the same lovely shade of amethyst as the other pieces to the set. I also own this set in the blue, and have seen the tray advertised in apple green. The coincidence of colors is startling to say the least. There is absolutely no doubt in my mind as to the originality of this tray, and I will back up this claim until I can be proven wrong—where after I will gladly print a retraction in this column at a later date.

The thing which makes this discovery so important is that the tray is script signed "Northwood" in the base, and this virtually cinches the original manufacturer of *Nestor*. It is also interesting that the stoppers in both cruets are what cruet collectors refer to as "Northwood faceted stoppers." This same mold stopper was also used by Beaumont and McKee Glass Companies, and can also be found in custard and chocolate glass.

Also of interest is the fact that we find *Nestor* in colors that match perfectly those in which *S-Repeat* was made. A few issues back I offered my contention that *S-Repeat* was introduced at Northwood's Indiana, Pa. factory. This theory can now be considered fact. This is due to one of this column's readers, who was nice enough to write me and confirm my daring speculation. Mr. V. T. Henry informed me that his uncle, who was employed at this Pennsylvania factory, gave Mr. Henry's mother a green *S-Repeat* toothpick holder which he brought home from work. My sincerest thanks to this reader for his confirmation of my theory, as well as to all others who have written offering important bits of information on other patterns, such as *Gibson Girl* and Consolidated's *Criss-Cross*.

A comparison of *S-Repeat* and corresponding pieces of *Nestor* will reveal startling similarities in pattern and mold characteristics. Undoubtedly they have common origins.

It is not known whether *Nestor* was made at The Northwood Company (Indiana, Pa.) or at H. Northwood & Company of Wheeling, W.Va.* Both of these plants were existing and operating at the same time, but Harry Northwood had sold out his interests in the Pennsylvania factory in early 1902. However, the plant technicians and decorators undoubtedly had acquired the distinguishable Northwood "touch", and undoubtedly many original Northwood molds. This interesting note appeared in a trade journal in June, 1904:

> "The Dugan Glass Works are manufacturing much the same lines . . . as are now made by Northwood at Wheeling. Mr. Northwood had established a great popularity for his . . . colored glass goods at the time he sold this plant to the National Glass Co. Mr. Dugan has maintained the quality of the famous ware and held much of the trade."

If *Nestor* was indeed made at the Pennsylvania site, then production was probably continued by the Dugan managers, who took over the Northwood factory after the absolvement of the ill-fated National Glass combine. This may explain the rectangular tray which has been reported to me on which the cruet set can also be found. I have not seen this tray personally, but the owner claims they are as certain of the originality as I am about the "Chrysanthemum Sprig" tray. This reported tray has no characteristics of *Nestor's* pattern in it either.

The *Nestor* pattern can also be found in a 4-piece table set (butter, creamer, sugar, spooner), the water set, berry set, jelly compote, and the cruet set (the toothpick was part of this set, and it is rare to find one of these decorated).

In closing, I want to present a plea to all who read this series. Any information which you may have access to which proves any part of this series to be incorrect is most important to all of us. I make no claims of infallibility. The final attribution and documentation of our beloved early glassware is so important to me that I gladly seek and accept any future or past reports which prove my own research findings to be flawed. Despite the superb work of pioneers like Kamm, Lee and Metz, glass research is still in its early stage, and there are literally thousands of unreported bits of data which need to be documented for future glass collectors. I urge all of you to share your own little discoveries with the rest of us. It is a crime to withhold the documentation of your findings from countless numbers of collectors.

*I am now relatively certain the pattern was made at Indiana, Pa., even though no definite shards in the pattern have been discovered at the factory site.

FIG. A—"Nestor" pattern decorated cruet (left) and undecorated cruet set (right)

FIG. B—Intricate design which is decorated on four of the eight panels of "Nestor".

"NORTHWOOD'S NO. 12

It may appear to my readers that I seem to lean rather heavily toward reporting on the unlisted patterns produced by the brilliant Mr. Harry Northwood. The reason for this is simple. Mr. Northwood was one of the few glass businessmen who managed to survive from the 1880s until the early 1900s, which was also the height of the Victorian era. He concentrated his innovative and experimental work primarily, but not exclusively, on the colored glass market. Since I am personally preparing an encyclopedia on the colored glass production of this era, naturally my research tends to uncover unreported facts concerning the products made by the man who led the field in production of quality colored tableware.

Whereas the name of Harry Northwood is well known to collectors of custard, of carnival glass, and of fine pattern glass in general, he has not yet received the credit he so richly deserves for scores of patterns which fail to carry his post-1905 trademark (an underlined "N" within a circle), and for some which do.

This week, I will be discussing a pattern which has been shrouded somewhat in mystery since it was first listed by Hartung as "Near-Cut" in her work on Northwood patterns. Her information concerning this pattern is considerably incomplete, and in some cases incorrect. I will attempt to clarify these misconceptions here.

Illustrated as Figure A is a reprint of a December, 1905 advertisement which appeared in an old trade journal I was fortunate to find. It illustrates a rather attractive imitation cut pattern, which resembles any number of similarly designed patterns from various companies who specialized in this type of pressed glass. However, it most decidedly was a "change of pace" for Mr. Northwood.

Hartung claims that the pattern was produced only in clear glass and carnival glass. However, my research proves the existence of "Northwood's #12" in emerald green, frequently with bright gold edges. Also, illustrated as Figure B, is a ruby-stained covered sugar and spooner. It was quite a shock and a thrill when I found these pieces recently, as they apparently disprove my own claim that Northwood never produced ruby-stained glass. At least it appears that way on the surface.

The only items previously reported in this pattern are a stemmed goblet, a stemmed compote, a 10" fruit bowl, and a flat plate. However, Figures A and B prove the existence of a table set, and I have personally seen a complete berry set, and have owned the salt & pepper in green. Dr. Peterson shows a crystal shaker in his book on salts, naming it "Locket." Undoubtedly a water set was also produced.

Hartung was right about one thing, however. This pattern obviously did not prove popular at its time of production, as it is very hard to find today. It is not easily recognized when seen, either.

The ruby-stained pieces illustrated are not signed with the Northwood trademark, which leads me to believe that perhaps an independent decorator purchased quantities of Northwood crystal for his own wholesale market.

Which brings us to the problem of what to call this pattern. In 1969 Hartung named it *Near-cut,* in 1970 Peterson called it "Locket" and now in 1975 we learn that it was originally called "Northwood's #12." I believe in the right of priority in naming patterns, but the Hartung name has only caused confusion concerning the Cambridge Glass Company's "Near-cut" trademark. Every time I advertised a piece of this pattern using the Hartung name, the inquiries would start pouring in. Thus, "Northwood #12" seems a fair compromise, as it *is* the original manufacturer's name—right?

FIGURE B—Very rare ruby-stained covered sugar and spoon holder in featured pattern.

FIGURE A—December, 1905 advertisement illustrating Northwood's #12 pattern.

"NORTHWOOD REGAL"

Beginning this month I am offering a new feature for the *Glass Review*, where I will focus on a specific pattern each month, giving information and values of all colors made.

Around 1905, Harry Northwood released a simple but beautiful table line which Hartung named Regal. The name she chose is appropriate but unfortunate, since there are already two other patterns carrying the Regal name. Thus, this line should always be referred to as Northwood's Regal to avoid confusion with the other patterns. Peterson, in his superb book on salt shakers, named this pattern "Blocked Midriff", but it is seldom used today.

Northwood's Regal is often found with the distinctive N-in-a-circle trademark which made it possible for us to attribute this pattern to it's original source. No early ads or catalogues have been found to confirm the manufacturer's dates, but the pattern was definitely made between 1905-1910.

Known colors are cyrstal and emerald green, often gilded. In opalescent, the line is found in white, green and blue opalescent, with touches of gold which is usually worn off. When I wrote my book on opalescent glass I was unaware of the existence of the cruet and celery vase in this line, both of which are very rare. Other items made are listed in the price report. No toothpick holder is known. The stopper shown in the cruet is not original.

NORTHWOOD REGAL

(prices quoted are for mint condition with good gold)

ITEMS:	Clear	Emerald Green	White Opal	Green Opals	Blue Opal
Water pitcher	$55	$150	$125	$200	$300
Tumbler	12	25	20	35	40
Covered Butter	45	100	100	175	200
Covered Sugar	35	65	55	100	125
Spooner	25	50	40	50	60
Creamer	20	40	35	50	65
Cruet (V.R.)	55	175	125	225	275
Celery Vase (V.R.)	45	75	75	125	150
Salt Shaker (Rare)	15	30	30	40	50
Berry, Master	25	50	50	75	120
Berry, Individual	8	15	15	22	26

V.R. = Very Rare

Very rare green opalescent cruet in Northwood Regal—stopper not original.

White opalescent tumbler and pitcher in Northwood Regal.

"OPALESCENT STARS & STRIPES"
Another Case of the NEW Versus the Old

Illustrated here is a water set so unique in design, in color, in appeal and in shape that it angers me deeply that its desirability among collectors has been hampered by reproductions which have infested the market. To this writer, the *Opalescent Stars & Stripes* pattern represents everything that we are striving for in preventing the outrageous duplication of glassware which should be a part of our heritage.

With the approaching Bicentennial, the timing is so absolutely perfect for passage of legislation requiring the permanent dating of glass which is made to imitate the old. Thus we would be preserving the first 200 years of glass production in America for all future generations of collectors. It would still make it possible for those who cannot afford the true antique to buy imitations—and with the glass dated, it will increase in value over the years as well. But it would also stop this miserable cancer which is knawing away at the investment power of our collections. I wish it were possible for me to reprint here some of the letters I have received from collectors who have been badly "stung" by reproductions, and the handful of poorly trained (or disreputable) dealers who are responsible for infiltrating these abominations into a healthy, but wary, market.

It is not the glass companies which are distributing these reproductions into the hands of collectors, but they do sew the seeds upon which this plague has spread. However, I can site one importer who blatantly distributes reproductions of true antiques directly into the hands of dealers of questionable integrity. We can be truly thankful that these money-grubbing opportunists' are few, and that collectors are more educated now than they have ever been before. Perhaps through public exposure we can lay bare the cheap imitations on which certain individuals hope to make a quick buck.

The water set shown here is the *real* thing, and so terribly rare that I couldn't even locate an example of the pattern for my recent publication on opalescent glass. Fortunately I did have an old catalogue reprinted in the book which included this set among its pages (shown here for your enjoyment). The set in Fig. A is in a lovely shade of cranberry opalescent. The pattern was also made in flint & blue opalescent. The only other items made to match were a barber bottle and a lamp shade. A cruet is known, but I cannot document it as being originally made without inspecting it first-hand. At least it is not shown in any of the old catalogues I have studied.

Opalescent Stars & Stripes was originally made by Hobbs, Brockunier & Co. (later the Hobbs Glass Co.) of Wheeling, W.Va. around 1888. This fine company was closed down shortly after its merger into the giant U.S. Glass Company. Somehow the molds were later acquired (circa 1895) by the Beaumont Glass Co. (operated by Harry Northwood's Brother-in-law, Percy Beaumont) of nearby Martins Ferry, Ohio, and re-issued. Their shapes are absolutely identical, the colors the same, and it would be virtually impossible to tell the Hobbs version from Beaumont's (see Kamm's, plate 59 for a reprint from the Beaumont catalogue). To this writer, it seems unimportant to differentiate the two, as they were made less than ten years apart from each other, and most likely by some of the same glass artisans. After the Hobbs closing, many of the unemployed glassmakers brought their craftsmanship and experience to other nearby factories.

This pattern has been reproduced since the 1940s, although it is not being made today to my knowledge. Except for the questionable cruet (it has a ruffled top & reeded handle and milky opalescence—all signs of newness) I know of reproductions in the tumbler (thicker than the old, with distinctive ribs on the inside top rim), the creamer (made from a tumbler mold—saw one without a handle once), and reportedly the barber bottle (although I personally feel that this piece was never reproduced).

The word "opalescent" should always precede the name of this pattern so that confusion can be spared, for there is a pressed glass pattern also called *Stars & Stripes*. The value of the set shown here is quite high, due to its rarity, due to the rising popularity of opalescent glass, and due to the Americana theme of the pattern.

FIGURE A—Rare Opalescent Stars & Stripes water set, made by both Hobbs & Beaumont Glass Companies.

FIGURE B — reprint of page from old Hobbs Glass Co. catalogue, circa 1888.

"OPALESCENT SWIRL"

Illustrated here are three blown opalescent tumblers in variations of the OPALESCENT SWIRL design. All three were blown into molds which are similar, but decidedly different. The tumbler on the left is in the popular "Chrysanthemum Base" pattern (name by Peterson). The tumbler in the center is in the "Reverse Swirl" mold (name by Boultinghouse). But the tumbler on the right is a mystery!

However, as I was preparing this column, I believe I solved the mystery. It appears that this tumbler is the one which accompanies the water pitcher shown in my Book 2, page 49 (Figure H). I called this pitcher the tankard version of REVERSE SWIRL, but it looks like I made an error in judgment there. The opalescent swirls run in the opposite direction of those in REVERSE SWIRL, so this pattern probably was made by a different company — or at least certainly a different time. The shape of the pitcher is identical to the "Ribbed Opal Lattice" tankard (Book 2, Fig. 243), and in fact the mold for that pattern tumbler is the same one used on our mystery tumbler on the right.

The opalescence swirls to the right on both the end tumblers pictured here, since both RIBBED OPAL LATTICE and CHRYSANTHEMUM BASE have been attributed to Buckeye Glass Company, Martins Ferry, Ohio, I believe our mystery pattern probably was made there also. However, it is extremely difficult to name makers on blown opalescent pattern glass, since so few have ever appeared in early company catalogues or journal advertisements. All attributions to date have been based primarily on heresay, speculation and instinct — a rather risky venture to say the least.

The tumbler on the right should heretofore be referred to as RIBBED OPAL SWIRL, as it should no longer be included in the REVERSE SWIRL family. The error in my Book 2 will be corrected in the next edition of that book.

"PALM BEACH"

Illustrated here is a very rare 8" plate in blue opalescent PALM BEACH which I failed to list in my Book 2 opalescent glass because I had never seen one. I knew a plate was made in crystal and color-stained crystal, but doubted it was made in opalescent. Does this mean a cruet and salt shaker can also be found in opalescent somewhere? They are known in crystal. How about it collectors—anyone among our readers have a cruet, salt shaker or even a celery vase in opalescent?

"THE PANELLED GRAPE PATTERN"

This week I am featuring a pattern which has become quite popular despite the tremendous risk presented by a massive number of reproductions infiltrating the market. The pattern is generally known as *Panelled Grape,* but as is usually the case with all popular patterns, it is also known as "Heavy Grape" and "Heavy Panelled Grape."

Reprinted here for the first time is an advertisement found in an early 1904 glass journal which reveals that *Panelled Grape* was originally called the "Number 507" pattern of the Kokomo Glass Manufacturing Company of Kokomo, Indiana. Kamm reported in her Book 3 that the pattern was made "as late as 1903" at Kokomo (referring to J. Stanley Brothers "Thumbnail Sketches"), but she—and all other pioneers in glass research—preferred to believe the glass dated much earlier. Millard dates it from the 1880s. Metz seems to confirm this theory. Lee failed to date the pattern altogether.

However, Kamm also claims that shards of the pattern were unearthed at the first factory of the Boston & Sandwich Glass Company, a report I am unable to confirm here. It is at least possible that the pattern was made there, and then copied later by the mold makers at Kokomo. I doubt that the original molds were still in existence.

Unfortunately, most of the pieces seen today are reproductions. It is difficult to tell age on this pattern, so new collectors should undergo careful study when purchasing. Apparently the pattern has been reproduced for many years, much of it by L. G. Wright.

One certain way of detecting age is that occasionally pieces of *Panelled Grape* are found with color applied to the grapes and foliage. These pieces were definitely made at Kokomo. The colors range from a pale green wash on the leaves to a pink and yellow on the grapes. Gilding is also occasionally found on the edges. The pattern is rare in milk glass.

Other than Mr. Brothers' early reports back in the 30s and 40s, very little has been written about the Kokomo Glass Company. Only two patterns, *Panelled Grape* and *Dewdrop & Raindrop,* were ever officially attributed to Kokomo. Apparently this company was originally a branch of the famous Indiana Tumbler & Goblet Company, and was founded in 1900. The factory burned down some time after the appearance of the advertisement shown here, and then was rebuilt in 1906 as the D. C. Jenkins Company. An undated catalogue from this company shows a *Panelled Grape* wine amid a grouping of other wine glasses.

The D. C. Jenkins Glass Company closed down during the Great Depression, in 1932, and perhaps the original molds for *Panelled Grape* were the ones used on the reproductions.

Care should be taken not to confuse this pattern for "Late Panelled Grape," which is rounder in shape. It is noteworthy to mention that the goblet shown in Millard, Metz and Lee as "Late Panelled Grape" is identical to one shown in the Jenkins catalogue. This only goes to show that patterns reminiscent of the 1880-1890 period could be produced with superior quality

after 1905 — and even the experts can be fooled into thinking it dates much earlier.

In addition to the similar "Late Panelled Grape," we find another pattern known as "Darling Grape" which has caused considerable confusion to date. The name for this pattern was provided by Millard and endorsed by Metz. However, Ruth Webb Lee includes a "Darling Grape" butter among her grouping of "Late Panelled Grape" pieces. Kamm goes the full route, calling the water pitcher illustrated in her Book 1 by the wrong name.

Here is the easiest way to tell the three patterns apart: PANELLED GRAPE: the grapes are at the base of the pattern in very heavy relief — many pieces are pedestal-based; LATE PANELLED GRAPE: a continuous weaving vine of grapes & foliage around the center of the pattern, in slight relief; DARLING GRAPE: the grape clusters & singular leaves hang down from a solid bar or rod at the top of the pattern. All three of the above are panelled, which is the primary reason they are confused for each other.

My next column will discuss Kokomo's #450 pattern, also shown in the ad reprinted here. This pattern has never been listed to date and I have some interesting data to offer you concerning it.

THE "PANELLED SPRIG" PATTERN

Again I find myself featuring a pattern made by Northwood (and associates) which to date has been virtually ignored by earlier historians of pattern glass. A few pieces have appeared in various publications, with each author naming the pattern himself. It had been called "Sprig", "Rib Sprig", "Creased Scroll" and "Panelled Three Vine", so in 1974 I took a combination of the most appropriate words and officially dubbed the pattern *PANELLED SPRIG* in my first book.

Very little was known about the pattern at that time. I gave it considerable attention thereafter, accumulating data on *Panelled Sprig.* Pieces were on display at the Wheeling Oglebay Institute, attributed to Hobbs, Brockunier & Company. However, this attribution soon came under suspicion in 1975 when several boxfulls of glass shards were unearthed at Northwood's Indiana, Pennsylvania factory dump site. Among these shards were many pieces of *Panelled Sprig* in all colors known.

The Hobbs attribution may have been based on local citizens or on shards found at the Wheeling factory site. But you must bear in mind that Harry Northwood re-opened the long idle Hobbs factory in 1902 and produced glass there for a quarter of a century. It is quite possible that he retained and reissued the molds in this pattern. Many of the items donated to Oglebay by the Wheeling citizens as "locally manufactured glass" have to be accurately dated before 1892 or after 1902 before the actual maker can be determined. It should also be noted that Northwood worked for Hobbs in

1884 and was directly responsible for the innovations which emerged from this factory at the time.

It is really difficult to offer sound "facts" concerning this pattern's origins when one has to deal so much in theory. However, we do know that the pattern was made in Indiana, Pa. I also can pinpoint production of the decorated pickle caster, as it appeared in a 1905 retail catalogue which was recently shown to me. Remember, it's only a theory, but I believe the pattern was introduced before 1900, with production continuing a few years afterward. The reasons for this earlier date are purely speculative, but the finial on the covered butter illustrated is the same one found on *Royal Ivy*, a pattern which dates well before 1900.*

Panelled Sprig was made in a wide range of shapes and colors. It was made in a four-piece table set, a water set, a berry set, celery vase, cruet, sugar shaker, salt shaker, toothpick holder, pickle caster and jam jar. Only the cruet and salt shaker have been reproduced—be especially wary of the rich dark cranberry color in these items.

Colors include crystal, cranberry, rubina (cranberry fading to clear at the base), apple green, pale amethyst, pale blue and milk glass. A few items were made in crystal with an opalescent lattice pattern in the glass. The rarest colors are the speckled finish pieces in crystal and blue. These pieces are often incorrectly referred to as Overshot glass. A blue speckled sugar bowl is illustrated as Figure C. Note the unusual cone-like finial which is unlike the finial found on the cranberry pieces.

Cranberry and Rubina are the primary colors in which *Panelled Sprig* was produced. Only an occasional sugar shaker, syrup, salt shaker, or toothpick can be found in the other colors listed. A water set, table set or berry set in anything but the two primary colors would be extremely rare.

Only the pickle caster has been reported with enamel decoration. On all other items, the alternating panels can sometimes be found with an etched fern spray.

Only a limited number of patterns were made in cranberry as complete table settings. Cranberry glass is of the mold blown, not pressed, variety, and this glass is very lightweight and easily damaged. Apparently it was always considered a quality item and used only on special occasions, as most pieces I have seen on the market today are in surprisingly good condition. It never ceases to amaze me that so much of this glass managed to survive the near-century since it was first made.

*The reproductions by L. G. Wright virtually confirm that this pattern was made at Indiana, Pa. This company acquired it's molds from that area.

FIGURE A — (left) Rubina Panelled Sprig covered butter and (right) enamel-decorated Cranberry pickle caster in original silver-plated frame.

FIGURE B — Very rare pale blue Panelled Sprig sugar shaker — only a few items have been witnessed in this color in this pattern.

FIGURE C — Rare blue speckled sugar bowl in Panelled Sprig — note the unusual finial.

THE "PETTICOAT" PATTERN

This week I will be discussing a pattern which has managed to become quite collectible without the benefit of a listing in Kamm, Metz or Lee. And yet it was not entirely overlooked by researchers in this field, for a salt shaker was illustrated, and the name for this pattern introduced, in Authur Peterson's volume on salt shakers. This pattern, called simply "Petticoat", is illustrated here in a few choice examples, a tankard water pitcher, a syrup jug and a cruet.

Since this pattern was not listed until 1960, very little information about it has been offered to date. No maker has been named, no listing of colors reported, nor has the number of table items available been compiled for collectors. I will attempt to remedy this situation here.

Petticoat was produced only in crystal and in a luscious shade of vaseline glass, frequently with gold decoration. No other colors are known (although this pattern would have lended itself well to ruby-staining). The vaseline color has become quite collectible among devotees of this unusual yellow-green crystal.

Naming the maker of this pattern was no simple feat. My research has turned up no catalogues, no overlooked trade journal advertisements, and no shards of the pattern have been reported at a factory site. With this in mind, I am forced to depend upon a couple of pieced-together clues, as well as my own personal instincts regarding color and pattern characteristics.

Thus, the facts listed below lead me to believe that *Petticoat* was made by the Riverside Glass Company of Wellsburg, W.Va., around 1902.

A. The pattern matches identically the shapes common to the "Radiant" pattern (Kamm 5, plate 5) which was advertised by the National Glass Company in 1901. This conglomerate owned and operated the Riverside factory. Except for the diamond-point design in the center, these two patterns are virtually identical in shape and size.

B. The color of vaseline and the shape of the tankard pitcher (illustrated as Figure A) are identical to the "Riverside" pattern (Kamm 8, pg. 35) which is another known Riverside Glass pattern.

Petticoat was made in a wide variety of shapes including the four-piece table set (butter, creamer, sugar & spooner), the water set, berry set, a syrup and cruet (see Figure B), a toothpick holder and a salt shaker. Two items which I have not yet seen or heard of include the jelly compote and the celery vase. Their existence seems likely, and they would certainly be considered scarce examples of this pattern. The stopper to the cruet in Figure B is original.

FIGURE A—Scarce tankard water pitcher in the
"Petticoat" pattern.

FIGURE B—Choice "Petticoat" syrup jug (left) and cruet with original stopper (right).

"PLUMS AND CHERRIES"
by William Heacock
Author of "Encyclopedia of Victorian Colored Pattern Glass," Volumes 1-5

Over the past five years this column has devoted considerable attention to the beautiful colored pattern glass made by the brilliant Harry Northwood, master mold designer, color experimentalist and business manager. His career lasted almost four decades, and his legacy is the hundreds of patterns and novelties which are eagerly sought by today's collectors. I have been working on a book for four years devoted to this man's genius, and just when I think I have everything together, another pattern or color turns up which makes me aware of how much more there is to be discovered.

This week I am pleased to introduce to glass lovers everywhere another unknown Northwood pattern which I am naming PLUMS AND CHERRIES. This pattern remains unlisted in all the early glass references, and just recently was reported in carnival glass (unfortunately called "Two Fruits", which was already assigned earlier to a Fenton relish dish). In order to avoid confusion with the Fenton version, I feel the name PLUMS AND CHERRIES should hereafter be the sole name for this pattern.

Northwood issued a good number of patterns after 1903 with cherries as a major part of the design. Some which come to mind are table settings in *Cherry Thumbprints, Cherry Lattice,* and novelties in *Three Fruits* and *Grapes & Cherries.* Fortunately, our featured pattern is easy to identify because of the cluster of plums on the reverse side of the pattern, as well as the unusual convex bulges along the base of most pieces.

Figure A clearly illustrates the "plum" side of the pattern in a water pitcher and tumbler. Note that the tumbler lacks the distinctive bulges.

Figure B illustrates the creamer to *Plums and Cherries* on the left and a similar creamer in *Cherry Thumbprints* on the right. The differences are obvious when the two are seen side by side, but since both are color-stained with similar clusters of cherries, the reverse side of the pattern must always be considered.

The *Plums and Cherries* pieces shown here have the distinctive Northwood trademark at the base of each piece—an N-in-a-circle, which dates the pattern some time after 1905. The line underwent limited production in color-stained crystal and is very, very rare in carnival glass colors. Only a table set, water set, berry set and celery vase have been documented in this pattern to date.

There seems to be some confusion also about another cherry pattern which Hartung calls *Cherry and Cable.* It is my opinion that this pattern is the same as *Cherry Thumbprint,* but the "thumbprint" portion of the pattern was eliminated on the tumblers, much as the bulges are eliminated from the tumblers shown here.

FIGURE A—Water pitcher and tumbler in rare PLUMS & CHERRIES pattern by Northwood.

FIGURE B — (Left) Creamer in PLUMS AND CHERRIES compared to (right) creamer in CHERRY THUMBPRINTS. Note the differences in the "cables", the cherry clusters and the designs along the base.

"POSIES AND PODS"
Another Unlisted Northwood Creation

Every time my continued research in this field turns up a Northwood tableware pattern which has not been listed, it is a distinct thrill to share these discoveries with readers of this column. It continually baffles me that there seems to be no end to these reports on Northwood—and I truly anticipate with relish each new finding yet to come.

Featured this week is a pattern which I have named "Posies and Pods" for obvious reasons. The pattern is really quite scarce, as I have only seen a half dozen pieces in the past four years. I felt strongly that the pattern "must" have been Northwood, but had no absolute proof, so I held off writing a column on it until now.

The reason this column can now be presented with some authoritative documentation is that the berry bowl illustrated in Figure B (left) has the distinctive Northwood trademark in the base—an "N-in-a-Circle."

Posies and Pods has all the Northwood characteristics for which his designs have become so popular among today's glass collectors. The ribbing and beading at the base of the water pitcher (Fig. A—right) are identical to that found on the "Jewel and Flower" water pitcher, popular in opalescent glass. The sandy stippled background is identical to that found on Northwood's "Blooms & Blossoms" pattern, recently featured in this column (see final paragraph).

The pattern dates after 1905 and was made at Wheeling, W.Va. Crystal and emerald green with gold are the only colors seen to date. Only a limited number of items were made, including a water set, a berry set and the four-piece table set (covered butter, covered sugar, creamer and spooner). No cruet, celery vase, toothpick holder or salt shaker have been documented to date.

It is quite possible that the pattern may have had limited production after 1910 in carnival colors, but these would without doubt be very very rare.

The *Posies and Pods* pieces illustrated in this column were loaned to me by two very devoted people, the Bowers from Michigan who searched more than five years to acquire the pieces shown here (as well as a creamer, spooner and a few small berry dishes). They collect no other glass, and it pleases me considerably that their apparently small venture into collecting pattern glass turned out to be one made by the glass genius himself, Harry Northwood.

And speaking of Northwood, I wish to thank all the readers who wrote me and sent pictures of the "Blooms and Blossoms" table set pieces. All were decorated with the multi-colored flowers, and it was truly thrilling to see these photos. This table set can now be confirmed. I also recently saw the large berry bowl which was acquired from a woman who stated her mother purchased it directly from the Northwood factory. How sad that so little documented data is available on this brilliant glassmaker's 40 year career.

My desperate efforts to find an early Northwood catalogue have met with dismal failure so far, but you can rest assured that I won't give up hope. Until then, I will continue to keep collectors informed of any new evidence concerning Northwood and his unlisted or uncredited production.

FIGURE A — (left) Posies & Pods tumbler and (right) water pitcher.

FIGURE B — (left) Posies & Pods signed Northwood berry bowl and (right) covered butter dish.

"THE PRISMATIC PATTERN"

It seems hard to believe that it was almost five years ago that I wrote my very first column in this series for the Antique Trader. Oddly enough, that first feature was about another pattern made by the little known Pittsburgh Lamp, Brass and Glass Company of Pittsburgh. Actually this company was a merger of three different factories, including Dithridge, the Kopp Glass Company and the Pittsburgh Brass Company. The company was formed around 1903.

P.L.B.&G. was known primarily for their fine production of lamps, in colors made famous by color genius Nicholas Kopp. I have mentioned Mr. Kopp frequently in this series, and have extolled his expertise in the field of colored glass production. My first column back in 1974 featured his popular Bead and Rib (or Beaded Rib) lamp, made in several colors including the red satin. Kopp formerly shared his considerable abilities with Hobbs and with Consolidated Lamp & Glass Co. Pittsburgh Lamp, Brass & Glass and Consolidated were strong competitors in the lighting glass field after the turn of the century, but demand for their production was greatly reduced by the coming of the electric age.

One thing which Mr. Kopp is not known for is pressed glass tableware, and this week I am featuring an early 1905 trade journal advertisement which contradicts that conception. I regret the quality of the reprint shown here, but the copying facilities at the library where this journal was found were primitive. Even though a portion of the advertisement was sliced, virtually every item in this line is illustrated. Usually these early ads showed only a representative sample from the line, not the entire setting.

The pattern was called PRISMATIC by its makers, a name which should be retained today, since I don't believe it has been named in Kamm or Lee. It is made only in clear glass and is a heavy and brilliant polished crystal.

The ad states that this line was "another of Kopp's great productions and is proving wonderfully popular." Whether this is advertising hype or not is a matter of speculation, but I have seldom seen pieces of this pattern in shows or collections, which leads one to believe production was somewhat limited. Perhaps the line did not sell as well as the manufacturers had hoped.

Prismatic has not been reproduced and represents a safe investment for those who are susceptible to its simple charm.

Pittsburgh Lamp, Brass and Glass Co., Pittsburgh,

The Prismatic "Idea" is new in Table Glassware. It is not an imitation, nor can it be imitated (Design being patented.) It is another of Kopp's great productions, and is proving wonderfully popular The Glass is clear and brilliant; each piece beautifully polished.

"RELIANCE" ASSORTMENT.

Consisting of —			PER DOZEN	
1/2 dozen	"Prismatic"	Sugars	$1.50	$ 75
1/2 "	"	Creamers	1.00	50
1/2 "	"	Spooners	.85	43
1/2 "	"	Butters	1.65	82
1/2 "	"	8-inch Berry Bowls	2.00	1 00
1/2 "	"	7-inch "	1.50	75
6 "	"	4½ inch Nappies	.40	2 40
1/3 "	"	9-inch Nut Bowls	1.75	58
1/3 "	"	9-inch Orange Bowls	1.75	58
1/3 "	"	10-inch Cake Plates	1.75	58
3 "	"	Individual Salts	.17	51
1/2 "	"	Oil or Vinegar Bottles	1.25	63
1/2 "	"	Syrups	1.75	88
3 "	"	Salts (Shakers)	.65	1 95
3 "	"	Peppers	.65	1 95
1/2 "	"	Pickle Trays	.75	38
1/2 "	"	Celery Trays	1.50	75
1/2 "	"	Water Bottles	3.50	1 17
1/2 "	"	Half-gallon Pitchers	3.50	1 75
6 "	"	Tumblers	.60	3 60
				21.96
		Package		1.25

NET COST OF "RELIANCE" ASSORTMENT, 27⅚ Dozen Pieces, $23.21

"PRISMATIC" HALF-GALLON PITCHER.

"PRISMATIC" WATER BOTTLE

"PRISMATIC" INDIVIDUAL SALT

"PRISMATIC" SPOONER.

"PRISMATIC"

"Prismatic"
Four-Piece Set.

"PRISMATIC" SALT. "PRISMATIC" PEPPER.

"PRISMATIC" SUGAR.

"PRISMATIC" CREAMER

"PRISMATIC" OIL OR

"PRISMATIC" SYRUP.

"PRISMATIC" BUTTER.

"PRISMATIC" 4½-INCH NAPPIE

"PRISMATIC" PICKLE TRAY

"PRISMATIC" 9-INCH NUT BOWL

"PRISMATIC" CELERY TRAY

"PRISMATIC" 7-INCH BERRY BOWL

"PRISMATIC" 9-INCH ORANGE BOWL.

"PRISMATIC" 10-INCH CAKE PLATE

"PRISMATIC" 8-INCH BERRY B

"RIBBED DROPLET BAND"
(Early Report)

What is the name of this pattern? Who made it? When was it made? These questions have been asked of me for years — and this column will offer little in the way of answers. For this covered butter dish is our featured "Mystery" pattern of the month.

I have devoted hours trying to trace the "roots" of this pattern, and only came up with a handful of clues. But first, I will tell you what I DO know about this pattern. I have seen it in the four-piece table set and believe it was also made in a water set and berry set. Most pieces I have seen had the unique petalled feet shown on this butter, a combination of frosted and clear glass, and a decoration of amber-stained vine-work, the latter identical to that found on occasional pieces of the "Zipper Slash" pattern. The finials on the butter and sugar lid are also frosted.

The name of this pattern? It is very similar to the "Petticoat Fluting" compote shown in Kamm's Book 8, page 77, but the finials are different. It is also similar to the goblet shown in Millard Book 2, plate 57, which he calls "Frosted Yellow Vintage." However, Metz includes this same goblet in her Book 1, re-naming it "Droplet Band" due to the fact that her example has no decoration. I could use the Metz name, but I don't think her goblet is the same pattern as this butter. Although it's hard to tell from the photograph, the goblet shown in Metz has a more zigzag effect, whereas our featured pattern has distinct ribbed bands. On the butter shown here these bands are found on the finial, just below the center of the lid and on the edge of the base.

But here is the real mystery — Metz lists bowls, tumblers and a water pitcher she has seen with the yellow vine-work. It seems to me that I also would have spotted a similar pattern if it existed, especially since I have devoted so much attention to it. So, if these patterns are one and the same, I feel safe in making only a slight variation of the Metz name by calling this covered butter "Ribbed Droplet Band." This way, if there IS another similar pattern, there will be some distinction between the two.

"RIBBED DROPLET BAND" dates around 1895. I cannot even attempt to name the maker, but the pattern is quite scarce and undoubtedly underwent limited production.

Ribbed Droplet Band covered butter.

Ribbed Droplet Band tumbler.

"RIBBED DROPLET BAND"

This week I am especially proud to present a real "exclusive" among my pattern glass reports. Despite the fact that this pattern has been seen many times in the past several years, I have been unable to find it listed anywhere in modern glass literature. Now the mystery is solved, thanks to the discovery of a rare early Duncan catalog which probably dates around 1887. These reprints are made available through the generous permission of Harold & Mildred Willey, and I think we all owe them a debt of gratitude. There are thousands of discoveries yet to be made in glass research, and it is people like the Willeys who make the answers much easier to find.

I have always referred to this featured pattern as *Ribbed Droplet Band* in previous reports, and there is no reason to attempt a name change here. It was the number 89 pattern of George Duncan & Sons, Pittsburgh, Pennsylvania, and I personally think it is one of their finest creations. Other lines featured in this catalog include the popular *Three Face* and *Baby Face* patterns.

Ribbed Droplet Band was made in crystal, frosted crystal and frosted crystal and amber-stained decoration. The amber-staining can be found on the ribbed bands and the grapevine design. The feet are usually frosted, and so are the areas around the grapevines. This combination of frosting and amber-stain reminds me of the popular *Klondike* pattern, and I see a big future for *Ribbed Droplet Band* inasmuch as its origins are now documented.

The unique feature about this pattern is the "tip-toed" feet, but as you can see from the reprint, not all pieces are footed. The covered butter comes with or without feet. The goblet, tumbler, salt shaker and many bowls and nappies are not footed.

Ribbed Droplet Band can be found today in shops and shows at reasonable prices, considering it is almost 100 years old. It has never been reproduced and represents a safe and sure investment for collectors who are wary of reproductions.

FIGURE A — Four-piece table set in previously unlisted RIBBED DROPLET BAND, circa 1887.

FIGURE B — Assorted compotes and bowls — note that the compotes come with or without covers.

FIGURE C—Undecorated version of **RIBBED DROPLET BAND**—the bottom portion of the goblet and the top of the unfooted butter were sliced from the copies.

"THE RING & BEADS PATTERN"
Custard Glass Update

Perhaps the single most rewarding experience of glass research is the opportunity to document those patterns and items not previously listed by glass historians. This week I will be offering information on a custard glass water set not listed to date.

I recently published a book on custard glass of the Victorian era which I had thought was relatively thorough. Needless to say, no research publication of any kind can hope to be a complete study. Continued research by myself and others keeps turning up new clues and eventual answers—the water set illustrated here attesting to that fact in my case. I can only be grateful for the opportunity offered by this column to keep pattern glass collectors posted on more updated findings.

This water set is in a pattern which Dr. Peterson referred to as *Ring and Beads,* noting that a small individual creamer and open sugar appeared in a 1915 catalogue of the Jefferson Glass Company of Follansbee, W.Va. In addition to these pieces, I listed a toothpick (the same mold as the individual sugar), a vase and a handled mug in my Book 4. These pieces are normally found with souvenir markings, but occasionally a rare piece is seen with floral decoration.

The pattern derives its name from the ring-like band and the row of beads found at the base of the tumblers shown here. However, the water pitcher is a unique form of free-blown custard (most custard glass is pressed) with an applied glass handle. The *Jefferson Optic* pattern previously discussed in this column also had a tankard shaped free-blown water pitcher, decorated almost identically with pink and red roses like those shown here. The difference in the two pitchers is that *Ring and Beads* has a ruffled top, whereas *Jefferson Optic* does not.

The Jefferson Glass Company first started producing custard glass around 1907, shortly after moving from its Steubenville, Ohio location to Follansbee. Other patterns made by this firm in custard include *Diamond with Peg, Ribbed Drape* and *Ribbed Thumbprint,* as well as dozens of novelty and souvenir items. Jefferson continued to produce custard glass as late as 1920, and apparently had considerable business associations with the "king" of custard production, Harry Northwood at nearby Wheeling, W.Va.

Ring and Beads also had limited production in crystal and ruby-stained crystal, primarily as souvenir items in the smaller novelties. Care should be taken not to confuse this pattern with the very similar *Washington* pattern, which also has a tiny row of raised beads at the base. The water set illustrated is extremely rare.

"RISING SUN"

Pressed glass was one of the earliest forms of tableware during the Victorian years of 1880 to 1910. However, very few patterns were so extensive as to include dinner plates as part of the setting. There are only a handful of the more than 5,000 early American patterns which can be found with a plate to the set.

This month I am featuring one of these few plates which is almost impossible to recognize, since it has few of the characteristics of the mother pattern. However, the inventory number 15110 identifies it as the plate to the RISING SUN pattern which was one of U.S. Glass Company's most popular lines. This plate was lifted from their 1909 catalogue, a discovery which should be especially thrilling to a collector of this pattern. The plate was made in both 6½" and 7½" sizes, and the prices quoted were wholesale.

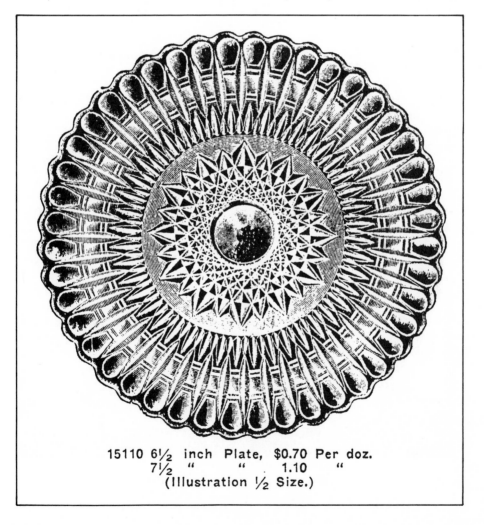

15110 6½ inch Plate, $0.70 Per doz.
7½ "   "   1.10   "
(Illustration ½ Size.)

"SERRATED RIBS & PANELS"

It seems hard to believe that when you combine the most important references of Kamm, Lee, Metz and Millard, there are still about 2,000 patterns which are not included. We have only scratched the surface in research on old glass, and so much more remains to be learned. In the past ten years, we have had some most important new information released by Dr. Peterson in his two books, by Revi in his mammoth publication on pressed glass, and by a number of recent catalogue reprints by others. It staggers the imagination when you realize that what we know now is only a fraction of what will be known in another decade.

This incredible new surge of data is becoming available due to the insatiable desire that collectors and dealers have for knowledge. We are no longer in the "dark ages" of knowledge, because researchers, authors and collectors are publishing books by the hundreds every year to meet the public's desire for more information.

I would be the last to criticize this new wealth of informative publications, since I am guilty of it myself. But I would like to exercise one word of caution. Because of the considerable investment one makes every year in reference material, certain precautions should be taken to investigate the validity of each publication. Ask dealers or other collectors which books they recommend for sound information. Investing in a poorly researched reference book is like buying a cracked piece of Lacy Sandwich. It may look beautiful on the surface, but your money would be better invested elsewhere.

Now, I'll get off my soap-box and share with you one of those 2,000 or so patterns which weren't listed in the early references. Illustrated here is a rare ruby-stained water set in a pattern I named *Serrated Ribs & Panels* in my Book 1. It is a quality glass pattern, made of superior, heavy crystal which glistens in the light.

A handled olive or relish dish is shown in this pattern in Barrett's book on ruby-stained pattern glass, but he incorrectly called it *Stippled Bar*. A quick check in Lee's "Victorian Glass" will confirm my correction of the name.

I rarely include columns in this series without naming the manufacturer, but this week I am afraid the maker of *Serrated Ribs and Panels* would be nothing more than a guess. The pattern dates around 1900, which means it could have been made by any number of glass companies known for their superior pressed cyrstal.*

Serrated Ribs and Panels was made in a limited table setting, including a water set (illustrated), four-piece table set, berry set, a toothpick holder and the aforementioned handled nappy. I cannot confirm the existence of a cruet, syrup pitcher or salt shaker at this time, but I am realtively certain they were made.

The pattern is known only in crystal, crystal with gold, and ruby-stained crystal. Any item in colored glass would be a singular rarity.

For collectors who are afraid of reproductions, our featured pattern represents a safe investment, as it has never been reproduced. It can also be purchased today at relatively reasonable prices, if you are lucky enough to find it, since unattributed patterns usually are not as much in demand as those whose makers are known.

*We now know the pattern was made by McKee Glass Co., circa 1902, as part of the National Glass Company.

"SIX-PANEL FINECUT"

Illustrated this month is a high-standard compote in a pattern which was named SIX-PANEL FINE-CUT by Don Smith in his book on Findlay, Ohio glass. It is indeed ironic that this good, old pattern was not listed by Kamm or Lee in their pioneer glass references. This compote came with or without a lid, and the pattern can be found in plain crystal and in crystal with amber-stained panels.

Also pictured is a portion of a rare 1890 Butler Brothers catalogue which offered several items in SIX-PANEL FINECUT. This catalogue makes it possible for us to date production of the pattern, but offers no insight into who actually produced it.

Shards of SIX-PANEL FINECUT were unearthed at the factory site of Dalzell, Gilmore & Leighton, of Findlay, Ohio, which closed its doors in 1901. It was Don Smith's discovery of these pieces of glass which made it possible to attribute much of what was made at all the Findlay factories.

It is often that this featured pattern is confused for the popular "Panelled Daisy & Button" pattern made by Duncan at the same time. In amber-stained crystal, the Duncan line was originally called Amberette. Even more ironic is that Dalzell, Gilmore & Leighton made a different pattern which they called Amberette (popularly known as "Klondyke" today). A recent publication on Pittsburgh glass even goes so far as to show pieces of SIX-PANEL FINECUT in a grouping labeled "Amberette".

SIX-PANEL FINECUT was made in a large table setting, including a creamer, sugar, spooner, and covered butter, a water pitcher and goblets, a berry set, covered high-standart compotes in two sizes, a covered bowl, plates, nappies, and a syrup pitcher. No toothpick, salt shaker or cruet have been reported to date in this pattern, and I doubt seriously that they exist.

This pattern has not yet reached the collectibility level it deserves. It is relatively scarce, but when found, usually can be bought for a bargain price. I have seen amber-stained water pitchers for less than $50, which is virtually unheard of in color-stained crystal. I have seen covered compotes for $50-60, and a butter dish for around $35. The pattern deserves much more value than this, and I think that it should be grabbed by pattern glass enthusiasts whenever found at these prices. It is my opinion that amber-stained SIX-PANEL FINECUT will rapidly increase in the next few years to three times the present relative value. It has never been reproduced, and represents a safe investment to collectors who are wary of reproductions.

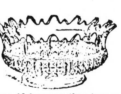

"SHELL" & "SHELL AND DOTS"

Illustrated in Figure A is a toothpick holder in the "Shell" pattern, which for years has been incorrectly attributed to the Jefferson Glass Co., at Follansbee, W.Va. Kamm book 7, page 58, labels this their #211 pattern, citing a rose bowl shown in plate 57 of this same volume. Figure B illustrates this #211 pattern, and it is obvious that the two are not the same at all.

Adding to the confusion, Mrs. Hartung's book on opalescent glass picked up on the Kamm error and also attributes "Shell" to Jefferson Glass. She correctly attributes the Figure B. rose bowl to Jefferson, naming the pattern "Shell and Dots," but fails to mention the double-pattern confusion. I have seen this early Jefferson catalogue at the Oglebay Institute in Wheeling, W.Va. (the reprints in Kamm are rather blurred), and can state with certainty that "Shell" is absolutely not the #211 pattern of the Jefferson Glass Co.

So, just exactly who did make this pattern? Design and color characteristics lean strongly towards Northwood as its manufacturer. The figural aspects of the pattern are reminiscent of his "Argonaut Shell" line, and his "Cabbage Leaf" and "Leaf Chalice" novelty vases. It is of major interest that the stopper and tray to the cruet set are the same as those found in the "S Repeat" pattern, which some sources feel is of Northwood origin (while associated with National Glass Company). Virtually binding this attribution is the later carnival line in "Shell" which is often found with the Northwood trademark.

Besides the carnival colors, "Shell" can be found in opalescent and non-opalescent colors of crystal, blue, green and canary yellow. Pieces of the pattern are very scarce today, and obviously had a limited run. I believe them to date sometime after 1902, with the establishment of Northwood's new Wheeling, W.Va. factory.

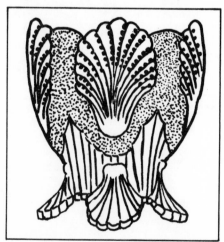

Fig. A—"Shell" pattern toothpick.

Fig. B—"Shell and Dots" Rose Bowl (Jefferson's #211).

"SPANISH LACE"

Spanish Lace is probably the most desirable and yet feared patterns in the line of mold-blown opalescent glass. Until recently, this pattern was thought to have been reproduced. We now know differently, for it is the similar "Daisy & Fern" pattern—sometimes incorrectly called Spanish Lace in price guides—which is the unfortunate victim of massive copying. Fenton did reproduce the design in a limited line of colored pressed novelties (cakestands, compotes, etc.) in the past ten years, but in opalescent glass, SPANISH LACE represents a surefire and safe investment.

The pattern is a Northwood design, dating as early as the 1890's, with continued production into the very early 1900's. Shards of the pattern have been found at Northwood's Indiana, Pennsylvania factory site.

The pattern was made primarily in white, blue, canary and cranberry opalescent. Green opalescent is rare. The prices quoted below are for mint condition.

ITEMS	White Opal	Canary Opal Blue Opal	Cranberry Opal Green Opal
Pitcher, squatty	$100	$225	$265
Pitcher, regular (see Cover Book 2)	115	235	285
Pitcher, tankard	135	250	300
Tumbler	25	35	45
Covered Butter (Scarce) (base is pressed glass)	85	175	250
Covered Sugar	60	100	125
Creamer	35	75	80
Spooner	40	75	85
Cruet (Scarce)	95	175	250
Syrup	120	225	275
Sugar Shaker	50	85	120
Salt Shaker (each)	22	32	45
Berry, Master	65	125	145
Berry, Individual	20	25	35
Barber Bottle (Scarce)	75	125	150
Cracker Jar (metal bail, rim and lid) RARE	100	225	285
Celery Vase	50	95	125
Water Bottle (Scarce)	75	125	175
Vase (assorted—some are English)	50	75	85
Rose Bowls	30	45	55
Perfume atomizer (V.R.)	50	70	95
Miniature lamp (V.R.) (base and shade)	225	350	450

A toothpick holder has been reported but never confirmed. The bowls can also be found in silver plated frames to make bride's baskets. Several of the above were never made in green opalescent.

Cranberry Spanish Lace cruet.

Spanish Lace barber bottle.

A REINTRODUCTION TO "S-REPEAT"

This week's featured pattern is also plagued by reproductions, which has created a fear among colored glass collectors who "just aren't sure" when they have an opportunity to buy the pattern. This wariness has clouded S-Repeat's appeal and prevented it from rising in value as rapidly as other colored patterns.

"S-Repeat" is one of the few patterns which isn't known by two or more names. It was named by Mrs. Kamm in her priceless volumes, and she reports that it was made by the National Glass Company. However, she fails to name which member factory of this big combine was actually responsible for production. The ad reprinted here (Figure A) was found by me in an early trade journal, and it too offers no clues to who made "S-Repeat."

The National Glass Company (est. 1899) was comprised of nineteen different companies. The big merger was plagued with serious problems from the outset and disbanded around 1904. However, I have found various catalogues which offered pieces of "S-Repeat" for sale as late as 1910, so the member factory responsible for production apparently did not meet with the same fate as National Glass.

So just who made "S-Repeat?" There is little doubt in my mind that it was first made at the Indiana, Pennsylvania plant of the Northwood Glass company. Except for my book, no other reference offers this assumption. This claim is not made without sufficient supportive data to back me up, and I will attempt to list these bits of proof here.

1. "S-Repeat" was produced primarily in colors of electric blue, apple green and amethyst (as well as crystal). These colors match to perfection the colors found in the "Nestor" pattern, which I am positive is a Northwood creation (more on this pattern in a later installment). Both of these lines were introduced around 1903. Actual comparison of these two bring so many identical characteristics to light that listing them here would be terribly space-consuming.

2. The tray to the "S-Repeat" cruet set is the same exact one used on the "Jewelled Heart" set, (See Fig. B). Both of these cruet sets were offered in a 1905 Butler Brothers catalogue. The "Jewelled Heart" set was offered to dealers in crystal, blue and green at 28¢ per set (cruet, salt, pepper & toothpick—all on a tray). The "S-Repeat" was offered in all four colors at 35¢ per set. Another pattern which this series earlier attributed to Northwood also had an "S-Repeat" tray for the cruet set. The pattern?—"Shell."

3. "S-Repeat" had limited production later (circa 1910) in carnival glass. A recent poll of various collectors and dealers in carnival overwhelmingly attributed this pattern to Northwood.

4. It is not well-known that "S-Repeat" had extremely limited production in opalescent glass. This author has only seen a half dozen pieces of this rare glass to date (tumblers, berries), and production was undoubtedly experimental. This shows a definite Northwood "touch", as his wares are

constantly turning up in colors and shapes completely alien to previously published listings.

5. The final clue which leads me to believe this is Northwood is the reproductions which have been made in this pattern by L. G. Wright Glass Company. This firm apparently has access to many priceless old Northwood molds, as they have also reproduced (in certain pieces) "Argonaut Shell", "Jewelled Heart", "Maple Leaf" and reportedly "Inverted Fan & Feather." None are marked with any form of permanent trademark unfortunately.*

"S-Repeat" has been reproduced recently in a goblet, a wine, a cruet and the toothpick holder, in colors of blue, amethyst and emerald green. The toothpick has also been reproduced in custard, ruby red, amberina and cobalt blue—all colors which were never originally made. There is no "sure-fire" way to tell a new piece of "S-Repeat" from old. I don't believe the goblet was ever originally made, but the wine was. Many of the original pieces were decorated with gold, so this would be a good way to determine age. However, many early pieces were also undecorated.

National Glass Company

Heeren Building, Penn Avenue and Eighth Street
P I T T S B U R G ,   P E N N A.

Fig. A.—1903 advertisement illustrating the "S-Repeat" pattern.

*Finally, and foremost, shards were discovered at the Indiana, Pa. factory site after this report was originally published.

Shard of S-Repeat salt shaker found at Indiana, Pa. factory site.

Reproduction S-Repeat cruet by L.G. Wright Glass Co.

"SWAG WITH BRACKETS"

While undertaking research for my book "The Encyclopedia of Victorian Colored Pattern Glass" I spotted a long-overlooked ad in an early trade journal that could be considered a find of major importance. This ad is reprinted here for your observation, and appears only mildly interesting at first glance. However, the jelly compote in the upper left-hand corner is in the highly collectable and well-known "Swag with Brackets" pattern which has heretofore remained unattributed.

Mrs. Kamm names the pattern in her Book 1, page 86, but offers no dates or manufacturer. Mrs. Hartung in her "Opalescent Pattern Glass" attributes it incorrectly to the Fenton Art Glass Co., of Williamstown, W.Va., circa 1907. However, the ad clearly identifies this pattern to be a product of The Jefferson Glass Co., at Stubenville, Ohio. This was found in a 1903 issue of the "China, Glass & Pottery Review", which dates "Swag with Brackets" somewhat earlier than Mrs. Hartung's contention.

The pattern was made in amethyst, electric blue and vaseline, usually decorated with gold, but is somewhat more popular in opalescent colors of crystal, green, vaseline and blue. The toothpick holder has been subject to reproductions for a number of years (reportedly by Degenhart). There are ways to avoid these reproductions, which are reported in my forthcoming series of books.

141

THE JEFFERSON GLASS COMPANY, STEUBENVILLE, O.

"TEARDROP FLOWER"
An Uncredited Northwood Masterpiece

Harry Northwood was a genius in the design, coloration and the business of marketing his creations. The name of this brilliant man is well known to collectors of his colored, opalescent, custard and iridescent (carnival) glass. In most cases, his glass has a distinctive quality and "look" all its own. And yet he has not been fully credited with scores of patterns for which he is responsible.

I personally have spent many agonizing hours in futile attempts at documenting his production from his early years as an employee of Hobbs Glass at Wheeling, W.Va., up to his final days almost 40 years later as the owner of the very same factory. No Northwood catalogue is known to exist at any of the dozens of museums and libraries through which I have scoured, or with which I have corresponded.* Thus, crediting Mr. Northwood with much of his production has sadly become a matter of piecing together clues, studying pattern detail and characteristics, tracing down dates of production, and using a researcher's "instinct."

This week I will be crediting Northwood with a pattern which has heretofore been overlooked by virtually every glass historian except Kamm. She named this pattern "Teardrop Flower" in her Book 7, and yet ruled out

*Recently a catalogue from the 1920's was loaned to me courtesy Fenton Art Glass Museum.

Northwood as its maker because it did not have his trademark. The only other publication where I found this pattern listed was Peterson's book on salt shakers where he unfortunately called the pattern "Flower & Bead." I consider this book one of the better researched books on glass available, and an occasional oversight in the re-naming of previously listed patterns is something that glass historians usually strive to, but cannot always avoid. I have done it myself—more often than I want to admit.

Our featured pattern is shown here in both the water set (Fig. A) and the 4-piece table set (Figure B). The water set is in a deep rich shade of amethyst, the table set in a light shade of green (almost, but not quite, apple green). *Teardrop Flower* was also made in a light shade of blue, and no doubt had some production in clear crystal. All pieces are found decorated with rich gold.

Attributing this pattern to Northwood with nothing more than a few clues could be risky, if it weren't for the fact that I am so absolutely sure. I will piece together these facts here, and perhaps you too will have no doubts concerning the origins of *Teardrop Flower*.

1. The color of amethyst is so rich that it can be compared to another Northwood pattern also found in this deep color. It is now known that the popular *Leaf Medallion* pattern was made by Northwood in 1903 (at Wheeling). A reprint of an original ad was shown in the Antique Trader in 1974, revealing this important discovery for the first time.

2. The handle on both the *Leaf Medallion* and *Teardrop Flower* creamers is identical. I have compared them personally and a line drawing is shown here for your observation (Figure C).

3. The general design of the pattern (the scalloped top, the arched panels, the basic shape) closely resembles *several* base designs of known Northwood patterns, like *Oriental Poppy, Singing Birds,* etc.—all dating after 1900.

4. The fact that the pattern is never found with a trademark means absolutely nothing. The Northwood N-in-a-Circle was initiated around 1905. Northwood opened his Wheeling factory in late 1902. This means more than two years of his Wheeling production remained unmarked. Also, not all of his post-1905 production was marked.

5. The following note appeared in a January, 1904 trade journal, referring to an exhibit being held by the various glass companies. *"Everything in the Northwood display is practically new. The Encore and Regent are regal looking patterns, in several rich colors, rich in heavy gold trimming."* The *Regent* line is the pattern we know of today as *Leaf Medallion*. Is it possible that the aforementioned "Encore" is the original name for our *Teardrop Flower*? Inconclusive, I realize, but an interesting theory.

Teardrop Flower was made only in the 4-piece table set, a water set, a berry set, cruet, and a salt shaker. No celery vase or toothpick holder has been documented to date. If they do exist (which I doubt, due to the post-1900 production cutbacks) then they would certainly be considered very rare.

Due to the fact that so little about *Teardrop Flower* has been reported to date, it can still be found (if and when you are lucky enough to locate it) at relatively fair prices. However, with this report of its origins, it won't be long before it joins the elite ranks of other sought-after patterns

Figure A—Scarce Teardrop Flower water set in rich amethyst with gold.

Figure B—Green with gold Teardrop Flower table set.

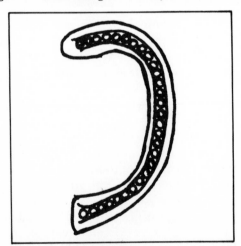

Figure C—Line drawing of beaded handle which is found on both "Leaf Medallion" and "Teardrop Flower" creamers.

"THE VENECIA PATTERN"

Glass research doesn't always prove to be as rewarding as I had hoped. Often, I come across an unlisted piece of glass, photograph it, and then place the shot in a stack with other pictures of undocumented early glass. Then begins an endless series of searches through source after source, hoping to come across some clue as to these patterns' origins. When these sources fail me, sometimes I go out on a limb and rely on my instincts. This is not a popular form of research, using theories instead of validated facts. Too many glass publications are on the market today with pretty much useless presentations of haphazard guess-work. Fortunately, glass collectors are more and more educated and can't be fooled into accepting anything but documented facts. I have talked to several who are even undertaking their own private research of their collections, and are kind enough to share the results with me for public presentation.

This week I will be "listing" but not attributing a pattern which has eluded me as to its origins. Illustrated are a creamer, covered butter and covered sugar in a pattern which I named VENECIA in my Book 3. The set (the spooner is missing) is in a lovely shade of cranberry glass, mold blown, with applied handle and finials. The base to the butter is solid crystal, and is original—not a match-up. Often mold blown pattern butter dishes had clear glass bases, especially if they were a plate or saucer-type base.

Venecia was also made in rubina (cranberry shading to clear), a lovely blown emerald green, and a most unusual green blending to clear. Other colors are probable, but these are the only ones I have witnessed to date.* The pattern was made in a four-piece table set, a water set, a berry set, a cruet, a syrup, a sugar shaker, a salt shaker and a toothpick holder. All pieces have the distinctive optic effect inside the glass, and are perfectly smooth on the outside.

Unfortunately, no maker can be named. However, *Venecia* deserves to at least have a proper listing and I decided to not delay this column any longer. The pattern dates about 1895 and is definitely American glass. Pieces with enamel decoration would be very rare, as I have seen none up to now.

The **VENECIA pattern**—a creamer, covered butter and covered sugar in a delicate cranberry color.

The pattern is also known in pigeon blood, usually enamel decorated. However, none of the other colors known have been found decorated.

THE WASHINGTON "STATE" PATTERN

Illustrated in Figure A is a rather scarce ruby-stained pint milk pitcher in a pattern which, despite its simplicity in design, has proved difficult for many glass collectors to identify. This is no doubt due to the fact that it is not listed in the works of our three major glass historians, Kamm, Lee and Metz. Neither is it illustrated in any of the lesser-known glass publications. Oddly enough, it isn't even shown in the Barrett book on ruby-stained glass.

Before 1974, the only place this pattern was illustrated was Warman's pattern price guide. He offered no pattern references, so it was with some hesitation that I listed the toothpick (shown in the Figure B assortment) in my first book as the *Washington* pattern, "reportedly part of the states series." Not certain about Mr. Warman's source for information, I hesitated being any more definite than that.

In 1975, glass enthusiasts were rewarded with a fascinating reprint from a U.S. Glass Co. Catalogue, to be found in Unitt's second book on goblets. This reprint confirmed Warman's listing, revealing *Washington* to be the U.S. Glass #15074 pattern. No date of production was offered, however.

My recent study of a priceless stash of U.S. Glass catalogues at the Carnegie Institute turned up additional documentation on our featured pattern. Kamm states that *Washington* was the last of the states series (Book 3, pg. 89) but also offers no date of production. The catalogue from which the reprint here was taken dates from 1910; however, I feel that the pattern was first introduced a few years earlier, and production continued for several years.

Washington was made primarily in crystal. However, Figure A shows that a ruby-stained version was made. It is quite scarce in this color. Not so rare is the "Wild Rose" decorated frosted crystal. This variation is machine decorated with a solid band of frosting and surrounded with flowers and vines. Finally, the rarest color is an ivory opaque glass, very much like custard glass (however, it lacks custard's luminous qualities). The ivory color was primarily used for souvenir ware, and would be scarce in unsouvenired tableware.

Obviously a wide variety of shapes were made in *Washington*. Besides the items shown here, I also know of a berry set, tumbler, salt shaker, celery tray & finger bowl. Note the many different sizes of drinking vessels, from the tiny cordial to the large-size goblet.

FIGURE A — Scarce ruby-stained 1-pint tankard milk pitcher in the Washington "state" pattern.

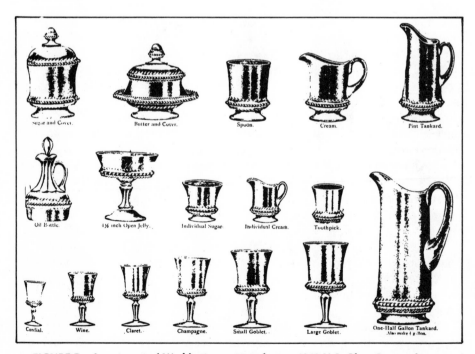

FIGURE B — Assortment of Washington pattern from a 1910 U.S. Glass Co. catalogue.

147

THE "WAVING QUILL" PATTERN

Although the title of this week's feature lists only one pattern, in a sense I will be offering my findings on two patterns. The tumbler shown here is in the "Quill" pattern, which is quite popular in carnival glass. The water pitcher I have named "Waving Quill", which you can see is very similar to the tumbler next to it.

Also known as "Feather and Scroll", our featured tumbler was part of a water set which is quite valuable in carnival colors of marigold and the very rare purple. *Quill* was also made in cranberry, emerald green and crystal — all usually with much gold. It is quite possible that the set can also be found in cobalt blue and "ivory" colored custard glass, but these have not been confirmed to date.*

The *Quill* pattern water pitcher, shown in the line drawing, is similar, but most decidedly different, from the *Waving Quill* pitcher shown in the photograph. However, it is my contention that the two shared the *Quill* tumbler as part of their water set. I have never seen or heard of a *Waving Quill* tumbler, and this pitcher was bought very cheaply with four accompanying tumblers, one of which is shown here. I doubt seriously that the two patterns were matched up by some enterprising dealer.

Instead, it is my theory that the *Quill* water pitcher, which is rather busy and quite Victorian in design, was replaced later by the *Waving Quill* which is more Art Nouveau in concept with its flowing design. Perhaps the manufacturers saw no need to create an entirely new tumbler for the new pitcher. Remember, this is only my own theory, and can be proved wrong if a tumbler exists in *Waving Quill*.

The *Waving Quill* pitcher shown here is in emerald green with much gold. It is light in weight, of the mold blown variety, with an applied handle. It is possible that a carnival glass water pitcher exists in this pattern, which would indeed be an extreme rarity.

The maker of the *Quill* pattern was identified in my Book 4, which illustrated and listed shards which were found at the Indiana, Pennsylvania factory dump site of the Northwood Glass Company. An easily identifiable piece from a tumbler was unearthed in emerald green. I am sure regular readers of this column, and all other true glass enthusiasts, share a deep appreciation to Del Helman, his father and special friends, all of whom took the time to seek out these shards and send them to me for study. Without these shards, many of my attributions would be merely speculation.

Since the *Quill* pattern dates after 1905, when Harry Northwood no longer operated the factory, credit for the making of *Quill* and *Waving Quill* should be granted to his Uncle Thomas Dugan, and the Dugan Glass Company. (Later the name was changed to the Diamond Glass-Ware Company.)

I have mentioned Mr. Dugan frequently in the column and will not be repetitious here, but I will editorialize just a bit by making the claim that it is about time the Diamond Glass-Ware Company received credit for the

beautiful carnival glass which came from their factory. Mr. Bill Edwards, in his recent publication on Northwood carnival, provided a mountainous service to all carnival collectors by listing the shards in carnival glass found by Helman, which he studied in my home in the summer of 1977. Many patterns long credited to Northwood can now be properly attributed to his equally talented Uncle.

FIGURE A—Emerald green with gold QUILL pattern tumbler and WAVING QUILL water pitcher.

FIGURE B—Line Drawing of QUILL pattern water pitcher (drawing by the late Rose Presznick).

*A reader has confirmed the existence of Quill in cobalt blue since this report first appeared.

THE "LATE WESTMORELAND" PATTERN

At the turn of the century virtually every glass company produced a pressed glass pattern to simulate the popular cut glass of the day. These new lines were naturally much cheaper to produce, and thus much more affordable to the Victorian housewife, and the glass remained popular for more than a decade.

This week's featured pattern, to the best of my knowledge, has not been reproduced to date. However, its popularity among collectors has been considerably minimized by two distinct factors. First, it is shown in Kamm, Book 7, in the ad and catalogue reprints in the back, but she failed to list it in her text or index. Secondly, the unfortunate name given this pattern was "New Westmoreland," and that first three-letter word can destroy any collector's faith in the age of this lovely glass.

Perhaps I am taking liberties here, but since I am the first glass historian to discuss this pattern in any depth, I personally prefer the pattern to be called "Late Westmoreland." Calling it simply "Westmoreland" would be confusing due to the fact that another pattern carries that same name, and it was introduced ten years before *Late Westmoreland* (by Gillinder & Sons, at Greensburg, Pa.)

Late Westmoreland is somewhat difficult to recognize on sight, perhaps due to its striking similarity to any number of imitation-cut pressed patterns. It is particularly similar to the U.S. Glass Company's *Pennsylvania* and *Minnesota*. The ad reprinted here was found by me in an 1898 issue of "Illustrated Glass & Pottery World." Also, the following note appeared in the January 13, 1898 issue of the "Crockery & Glass Journal," apparently referring to our featured pattern.

"The Westmoreland Glass Co. displays a new line of cut glass design in crystal and green, also some with gold decorations."

It should be noted that the Westmoreland Specialty Company was a subsidiary of the parent glass factory.

The set shown in the photo reprinted here is in a totally unique and lovely deep shade of bluish green, almost a "peacock blue," with rich gold decoration at the rim. *Late Westmoreland* was also made in crystal and is rare in milk glass. Westmoreland Glass specialized in opaque glass at the turn of the century.

To date, the only pieces which I can document in *Late Westmoreland* are the four-piece table set (butter, creamer, sugar & spooner), the cruet shown here (the stopper is original), a toothpick holder, and a salt shaker. Other likely items would be the water set and berry set.

1898 Advertisement featuring the "Late Westmoreland" pattern.

THE "WINSOME" PATTERN

Although this week's featured pattern is not a hot "scoop" for this column (it was discussed in a 1975 *Spinning Wheel* article), you won't be able to find it listed in any of the early references on pattern glass. In fact, I named the pattern first in my book "1,000 Toothpick Holders" when I was unable to find a name for it. Hereafter, this little-known table setting should be referred to as the WINSOME pattern.

Winsome first appeared in a February, 1903 issue of "Glass & Pottery World." It was featured in a full-page advertisement of the National Glass Company, and was listed as the Number 550 set made by member factory Riverside Glass Works, Wellsburg, W.Va. The National Glass Company was a major merger of 19 different factories with a total output from about 560 pots. Compare this to the "measly" 255 pots held by the competing merger United States Glass Company. It almost staggers the imagination that such a glass manufacturing empire could fail dismally in a quick four years.

The reasons for this incredible failure are many: a dwindling market for pressed glass tableware, dissension among their managers (including H. C. Fry and Harry Northwood) who eventually left National to create competing factories, several fires and floods, massive new construction when the

market could not bear more output, and other poor investments, like the factory exhibit at the Pan-American Exposition in Buffalo, New York. By 1904, the National became a holding company, leasing out its remaining factories to plant managers. By 1907, the firm went into receivership and became nothing but a bad memory for the enterprising glass wizards who dreamed of the biggest glass company in the world.

The *Winsome* pattern was made only in clear glass, sometimes with gold decoration. No colored glass version of the pattern has been reported to date. I seriously doubt colored pieces exist, even though Riverside was known for rich and beautiful colors. They are the makers of the very popular *Croesus* and *Empress* patterns. *Winsome* is relatively scarce, as I have only seen a limited number of pieces in several years. Demand for the pattern is low at the present time, but now that the line has been named and properly attributed, collectibility should increase.

National Glass Co.
Pittsburg, Pa.
Operating the following factories:

Beatty-Brady Glass Works, Dunkirk, Ind.
Cumberland Glass Works, Cumberland, Md.
Fairmont Glass Works, Fairmont, W. Va.
Indiana Tumbler & Goblet Works, Greentown, Ind
McKee & Bros. Glass Works, Jeannette, Pa.
Northwood Glass Works, Indiana, Pa.
Ohio Flint Glass Works, Lancaster, O.
Riverside Glass Works, Wellsburg, W. Va.
Rochester Tumbler Works, Rochester, Pa.
Royal Glass Works, Marietta, O.

No. 550 Set. Made by the Riverside Glass Works, Wellsburg, W. Va.

We are showing samples of new lines of
Table Glassware,
also of
Colored Goods,
and a large line of
Decorated Lamps,
at our different Sample Rooms

No. 550 Set. Made by the Riverside Glass Works, Wellsburg, W. Va.

No. 550 Set. Made by the Riverside Glass Works, Wellsburg, W. Va.

Branch Offices:

BOSTON, 144 High Street.
NEW YORK, 25 West Broadway.
PHILADELPHIA, 1107 Market Street.
PHILADELPHIA, 922-924 Market Street.
BALTIMORE, Cor. Baltimore and Hanover Sts.
BALTIMORE, 5 and 7 W. German Street.
CHICAGO, 45 E. Randolph Street.
DENVER, 1617 Lawrence Street.
SAN FRANCISCO, 578 Mission St.
LOS ANGELES, 340 N. Main St.
ST. LOUIS, 423 N. Fourth St.

No. 550 Set. Made by the Riverside Glass Works, Wellsburg, W. Va.

MISCELLANEOUS COLUMNS

On the following pages are a number of columns, features and "featurettes" which do not pertain to pattern glass, or which cover a variety of patterns making it impossible to classify alphabetically in the front section. Most of these appeared in the GLASS REVIEW after I became Senior Editor in 1979. My earlier columns for this magazine, which appeared on an irregular basis, were reprinted in "The Best of Glass Review", Volume 3, published in 1980. This book can be ordered from the Glass Review at Box 542, Marietta, Ohio, 45750. The price is $6 postpaid.

Featured in this section is everything from art glass to pattern glass, including lamps, cut glass, figurals, novelties, just about anything unusual in glass discovered during my research.

CATALOGUE REPRINTS

In addition to the catalogues recently rediscovered, I am pleased to announce that a choice 1928 Butler Brothers wholesale catalogue has been found. This month I am reprinting one of these pages for your enjoyment.

Butler Brothers was a gigantic outlet for many glass factories who wished to distribute their products as widely as possible. Unfortunately, this catalogue offers almost no information concerning the manufacturers of each of the lines of stemware, but the two lines at the bottom of the page are definitely Tiffin Glass in the "Classic" and "Bluebell" etchings. Not much is known about the production of the Tiffin Glass Company of Tiffin, Ohio, especially during the thirties and forties. However, one of our staff editors, Fred Bickenheuser, has been conducting research on this company for many years and has a considerable amount of data to offer us in coming months.

This month I am again featuring a page from my previously unlisted 1928 Butler Brothers catalogue. Illustrated among the several offerings are assortments from Fenton (top center), Westmoreland (top right), Imperial (center row right) and others.

However, my reason for featuring this page is the grouping at the top row left. Many of the items in that group are often attributed to Northwood, among them the COINDOT compote, the TWIG vase, the QUESTION MARK compote, and the WINDFLOWER bowl. However, the Northwood factory in Wheeling was no longer operating in 1928. This group of iridescent novelties offers additional proof that the Diamond Glass-ware Company, Indiana, Pa., was a major manufacturer of carnival glass. Glass shards have been found at the Diamond factory site in several of the patterns shown in that group. It makes you stop and wonder sometimes how many other long-forgotten glass factories produced some of today's more sought-after patterns.

It is interesting to note that iridescent glass was fast disappearing from the market at this time, and by 1930 it seems to have disappeared altogether, only to make a rare occasional appearance during the depression.

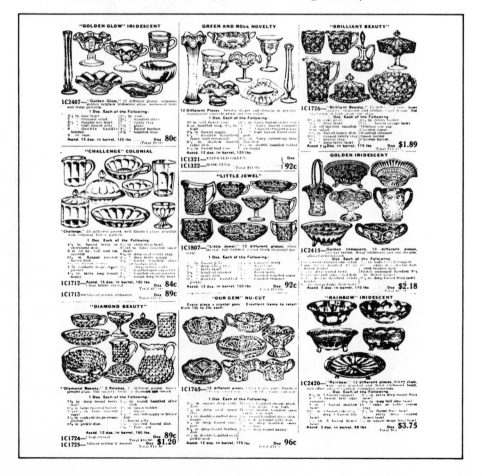

"CZECHOSLOVAKIAN ART GLASS"

Many of us have heard of the Czechoslovakian art glass from the 20's, but there has been almost no documentation concerning this glass to date. Reprinted this month is a page from a 1928 Butler Brothers catalogue which documents many of the shapes imported into this country in the late twenties. Notice especially the unique designs and shapes in this little-known hand-made glassware. Czechoslovakian glass is known for its especially bright colors (usually a spattering of bright yellow, reds, blacks and greens), and for gaudy applied flowers and rigaree. These brightly colored vases, bowls and baskets retailed to the consumer for less than $1. Today they are fast becoming collectible, and values are rising rapidly.

Art glass wares are favored gifts—here are two pages of most unusual gift pieces—they belong in your holiday line

Art Glass From Czecho-Slovakia

60 pieces in this assortment—and NO TWO ALIKE
A wonderful selection of artistic, decorative pieces to retail at 50c, 75c and $1.

1C6100— *60 pieces*, all different, made in Czecho Slovakia. A variety of artistic shapes in bright solid and mottled colors. Some have applied floral decorations in relief. Many are of the expensive double "cased" glass—all are hand made. The assortment comprises vases, some footed, handled baskets, flower bowls, covered boxes, flower holders with perforated metal tops, etc. Space does not permit our showing all pieces but those pictured are representative of the entire assortment. Asstd. 5 doz. in case, 100 lbs. (Total for Asst $19.75) DOZ **$4.20**

Czecho-Slovakian Double or "Cased" Glass

50 Beautiful Pieces—NO TWO ALIKE
A group of rarely attractive pieces of art glass to retail at $1.00 to $2.50 each.

1C6101— *50 pieces*, all different, in a variety of artistic shapes, both useful and ornamental. All in the popular bright tango and mottled colors with contrasting colored handles, feet, etc. *All extra large size pieces!* The assortment comprises handled vases, footed fruit bowls, candy jars, puff boxes, flower holders with perforated metal tops, handled baskets, etc. The illustration is representative of the assortment but the actual pieces must be seen to be appreciated! Asstd. 50 pcs. in case, 100 lbs. (Total for Asst $32.50) EACH PIECE **67½c**

FOSTORIA TABLE SETS

This month I am sharing with *Glass Review* readers a page from a rare, previously unknown Fostoria Glass Company catalogue for the 1899. It illustrates two four-piece table sets not included in the two available Fostoria reprints now on the market. Neither set has been named in pioneer references on pattern glass, nor were any other table items made in either pattern, so they should be referred to simply as Fostoria's #551 and #553 patterns. The same basic shape and mold characteristics were used on both sets, made only in clear glass.

ALL OUR WARE IS GOOD WEIGHT AND EXTRA FIRE POLISHED WITH NATURAL GAS, EXCEPT WHERE NOTED.

FOSTORIA GLASS CO.

CATALOGUES ILLUSTRATED

One of the single table items which represents the luxury of Victorian era dining is the pickle caster. Can you think of any other more superfluous way of serving grandma's homemade pickles?

Illustrated here is a page from the Rockford Silver Plate Company of Rockford, Illinois. If this catalogue were undated, I would guess it was published around 1900. However, it is dated 1910, a year when Victorian elegance was on a down-slide. Table items like butter pats, toothpick holders, sugar shakers, oil cruets and syrup pitchers were produced at a fraction of the quantity in which they were made ten years before.

The three cyrstal glass inserts shown here were purchased by Rockford from the Fostoria Glass Company. The No. 704 and No. 904 casters have EDGEWOOD pattern inserts. The No. 705 caster has a CZARINA pattern insert. The No. 404 and No. 689 casters have cranberry INVERTED THUMB-PRINT mold-blown inserts. You will note that this color of glass was known as "Ruby" glass at the turn-of-the century. The makers of the colored glass inserts are not known, as no clues are offered in the Rockford catalogue concerning their origin.

CUT GLASS

In an 1898 trade journal, these three gorgeous pieces of brilliant period cut glass were featured with the following promotional notes:

"Among the many new shapes and designs in cut glass just placed on the market by L. Strauss & Sons are some new features in bowls, jugs and vases, for which design patents have been granted. The bowls show a new combination which decidedly enhances their brilliancy.

"The jugs are new in cutting and shape. They have funnel-shaped tops and possess the special feature of having an additional cutting on the inside at the tops."

The Strauss name is not often thought of when collectors discuss the great manufacturers of rich cut glass, but the items shown here attest to the fact that their cutters were among the best in the trade.*

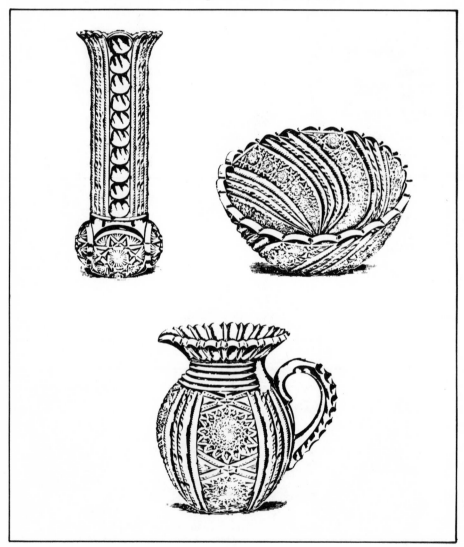

CUT GLASS

Featured here are three unique pieces of choice cut glass with silver mountings which appeared in a 1900 issue of "China, Glass & Pottery Review." These were products of L. Straus & Sons of New York, N.Y., manufacturers of rich cut glassware at the turn of the century. An article featuring these pieces stated that the company did its own mountings, which bore the Straus trademark. Usually this type of product was offered by silversmiths, who purchased finished pieces of cut glass from cutting shops. But according to this article, the increased rivalry in the cut glass market brought the prices down to such a point that the silversmith cut down on the quality of glass purchased in order to make a profit. It is fascinating to study a piece of Brilliant period cut glass and realize that every single groove was cut by hand with such precision that it staggers the imagination.

CRACKER JAR. PANTHEON CUTTING.

THREE-HANDLED LOVING CUP. LAFAYETTE CUTTING.

FRUIT OR SALAD BOWL. GOLDEN ROD CUTTING.

DUNCAN GLASS

Reprinted this month is a page from the 1891 catalogue of the United States Glass Company — Factory D. This page was not included in my Book 5, due to space limitations and is reprinted here for your enjoyment. Note the line of barware at the top, which is identical in design to a line also made by the King Glass Company (see my Book 1, Figure 261) and the Heisey Glass Company. Also note the unusual miniature (night) lamp in Duncan's No. 336.

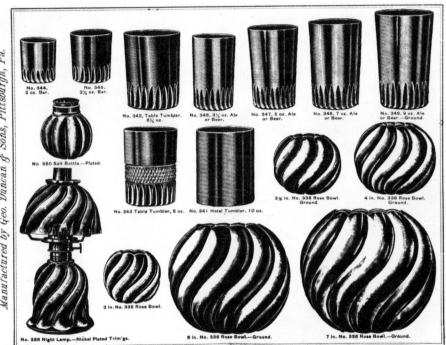

Manufactured by Geo. Duncan & Sons, Pittsburgh, Pa.

No. 344, 2 oz. Bar.

No. 345, 2½ oz. Bar.

No. 342, Table Tumbler. 8½ oz.

No. 346, 3½ oz. Ale or Beer.

No. 347, 5 oz. Ale or Beer.

No. 348, 7 oz. Ale or Beer.

No. 349, 9 oz. Ale or Beer.—Ground.

No 350 Salt Bottle.—Plated.

No. 343 Table Tumbler, 8 oz.

No. 341 Hotel Tumbler, 10 oz.

3½ in. No. 336 Rose Bowl. Ground.

4 in. No. 336 Rose Bowl. Ground.

3 in. No. 336 Rose Bowl.

No. 336 Night Lamp.—Nickel Plated Trim'gs.

6 in. No. 336 Rose Bowl.—Ground.

7 in. No. 336 Rose Bowl.—Ground.

CUSTARD GLASS RARITY

How delightful to have the opportunity now to share my correspondence with all of you. As much as I hate to admit it, I rarely have the opportunity to answer the hundreds of letters I receive every year from bewildered collectors. Most often, it is a matter of time. Sometimes I do not know the answer to their questions, or it takes too much time to try to look up the answer. I put these letters into a pile with the word REPLY written across the front, but with book production, photography schedules, column deadlines and my travels, these stacks of mail grow higher and higher and all my good intentions to answer these letters seem an impossibility.

A custard glass collector from Illinois wrote to me two years ago and enclosed this photograph of a cologne or barber bottle in light custard colored glass. He stated it was 10½ inchs tall with the stopper and about 4 inches in diameter. It has touches of worn gold paint and glows under a black light. He was curious who made this bottle and what it was worth.

I cannot be definite about the answer, but I believe the bottle was part of a line made by McKee Glass Company about 1902. The color matches their Geneva custard, and McKee was known for chocolate glass — a color in which this bottle can also be found.

This barber bottle is shown in Measell's book on Greentown Glass without a stopper. He states that it was not made in Greentown but was of interest only because of the production in chocolate glass. It is indeed quite rare in this color. It would also have to be considered scarce in custard glass with an estimated value of around $150.

*This "cologne bottle" appeared in a McKee catalogue for 1900, called "Venetian". Trays of various sizes and jewel boxes were also made.

THREE POPULAR CUSTARD PATTERNS
Courtesy of Harry Northwood & Associates

It is somewhat ironic that the two most expensive forms (or types) of pattern glass are not the oldest. It is not how old something is which determines its value, but how collectible it is. Thus we find that custard glass, which first appeared in this country around 1897, and "carnival" glass (1907-1920s), are frequently bringing astronomical prices in the rarer shapes and patterns.

It is generally agreed that the brilliant Harry Northwood first introduced this creamy opaque glass to the American market. A very similar English custard ware dates slightly earlier than Northwood's, and it is known that Mr. Northwood was frequently influenced by his English heritage and brought back many ideas from his not infrequent trips abroad. In all justice however, he improved on everything he copies, and his innovations and experimental production far outweighed his occasional lapse into imitating his competitors.

Northwood failed to patent the formula for custard ware (perhaps because it wasn't his in the first place), so a wide-open market was born for this new glass. It wasn't long before other companies—Heisey, Tarentum, Jefferson and later Cambridge, jumped on the bandwagon and offered their own versions of custard glass.

There are only a couple of dozen patterns available in custard glass table ware. Most assuredly, there are scores and scores of novelties and bowls of every shape and size (just as there are in carnival glass). However, when I refer to "pattern glass," I imply those pieces which were sold as table serving pieces, using a distinct design which is common to the entire setting. Novelties were frequently sold for a dime in local dry-goods stores, or were given away as premiums or prizes by local merchants, and those so-called "candy bowls" (a misnomer by modern standards), were stretched, ruffled, flattened and pulled into all sorts of shapes. But they came from a single mold, and should not be referred to as "pattern glass."

Illustrated here are three of the most popular and expensive custard glass toothpick holders known to exist. To date, all three of these patterns have been attributed to Northwood as mere speculation only. No writer seemed to have any proof. It is somewhat anticlimactic that I will both confirm and deny certain theories concerning these three patterns in this week's column.

NORTHWOOD'S MAPLE LEAF

The toothpick illustrated on the left is terribly rare. In fact, Hartung failed to even list it (or the salt shaker & jelly compote) in her publication on Northwood glass. These three shapes are *extremely* valuable, and yet it is ironic that the table set, water set and berry set are not, and are competitively priced with other custard patterns. Again we find a case where collectibility and rarity determine value.

It will come as somewhat of a major surprise to serious collectors of quality glass—but this pattern was also made in a cruet in custard. Only a few were apparently made, and the only one I know of is damaged, so anyone who has this cruet in their possession can consider themselves fortunate.

Kamm named this pattern in her Book 5, and based her attribution on unmistakable Northwood characteristics. I concur fully with her theory. It is only unfortunate that she could not have picked a less confusing name for this pattern, as there are no less than *three* other *Maple Leaf* patterns from different periods of production. Thus, the Northwood name should always precede the pattern name to avoid confusion.

Dating this pattern appears to be a matter of conjecture. Kamm avoids dating the custard, but states that the carnival version of this pattern was offered in a Sears catalogue in 1912. Hartung also fails to provide a date. The molds for the table, water, and berry set were later reissued in carnival colors, and the jelly compote was even issued as a novelty in opalescent colors of white, blue and green. The toothpick salt shaker & cruet were made *only* in custard.

A few shards found at the Indiana, Pa. factory site leads me to believe that the molds were retained and reissued by the Dugan Glass Company. In fact, it is possible the pattern was introduced after Northwood left the company in 1901.

WILD BOUQUET

The toothpick shown in the center is perhaps the rarest of all three, and yet existing price guides underrate it far too much. The pattern was never listed by Lee or Kamm, but Mrs. Metz provided the most-often used name "Wild Bouquet" in 1958. However, as is often the case, this little gem is also known by another name, "Iris" (especially by custard collectors).

Wild Bouquet was made in a table set, water set, berry set, toothpick, salt shaker, cruet and jelly compote. Hartung states that it was made only in custard glass, but it is generally known that a complete service is also available in opalescent colors of white, blue & green. I have received a bona-fide report that *Wild Bouquet* was also made in canary opalescent. To call this color rare would not do it justice. It belongs in a museum.

In custard glass, the table set can be found with a standard finial or with looping arches or bars which serve as a grip on the butter and sugar lid. The value of this variant is usually 50% higher than the standard finial version.

A few pieces of this pattern have been seen in non-opalescent colors. This includes the salt shaker and toothpick. Sometimes the opalescent is very deep and rich, sometimes its only a touch of white at the top rim.

Hartung was able to date this pattern from its appearance in an old ad she is fortunate to have found. This date is 1902. Actual location of production thus becomes debatable, as there were two companies carrying the Northwood name at this time. The Northwood Company at Indiana, Pa., was a part of National Glass Company. However Harry Northwood himself had pulled out of this firm over a year before and established his own factory, H. Northwood & Company at Wheeling, W. Va. in the fall of 1902.

So where actually was *Wild Bouquet* made? The answer is only half known. It *is* a definite fact that this pattern was made at Indiana, Pa. Thanks to Mr. Helman and friends, and the boxes of shards dug up at the plant site there, I now have in my possession three distinct pieces of this pattern in custard glass. However, there were none in any other color, so it is possible that Mr. Northwood retained the molds and continued their production at his Wheeling site. Some answers will never be known, but all theories must be investigated.

INVERTED FAN & FEATHER

According to Dr. Peterson, the name for this pattern was provided in some long out-of-print book on Milk Glass. It was never included in Kamm, Metz or Lee, which would lead one to believe that it is either terribly rare, or that those three pioneers thought it unworthy of inclusion in their books. These conjectures are both far from the truth. *Inverted Fan & Feather* was made in no less than five different types of glass—emerald green crystal, custard glass, pink slag, opalescent colors and limited carnival. Certainly some colors are rare, but others should not be classified as that.

Inverted Fan & Feather was made in a wide variety of shapes, including the table set, water set, berry set, toothpick, salt shaker, cruet, jelly compote, punch bowl & cups, and novelties of all shapes (pulled from the spooner mold).

The pink slag pieces have apparently broken down the barriers between collectors of art glass and collectors of fine pattern glass. I have frequently said that the reason patterns like Holly Amber, Libbey's Maize and the pink slag *IF&F* are commanding such tremendous prices is that they were lucky enough to get listed in an art glass publication. And yet they *are* pressed glass, produced with as much care as dozens of other equally lovely patterns (and some much, much rarer). I don't mean to undermine the value of those elite three—I just want to point out that the line between art glass and pattern glass is thin indeed (especially among the blown & mold blown patterns).

To date, attribution of *IF&F* has remained nothing more than mass-acceptance that it is Northwood. Hartung lists it as Northwood, but is unable to substantiate actual production dates. I have seen salt shakers with the blocked letters "Northwood" spelled backwards on the base, so we can be pretty certain that this is indeed Northwood glass. But again—which Northwood? I have several shards in this pattern which were unearthed at Indiana, Pa., including two big pieces in pink slag. Is it possible that this was never made at the Wheeling location? This writer personally feels that *IF&F* was introduced around 1899 (while Northwood was still very much involved with this company), and production was continued long after he departed. The name of the company was changed to the Dugan Glass Works around 1904, and it is ironic that this factory became one of Northwood's biggest competitors in the colored glass market, and even outlasted his own Wheeling firm by more than ten years.

The toothpick shown in this pattern was originally made only in the custard and the pink slag. It has been reproduced in both of these colors (and others not originally made) but fortunately the premium value of the originals has not been undermined, as there are distinct differences between the old and the new. Other reproductions in this pattern have appeared on the market in recent years. There has been some speculation in the past that the rose bowls, candy bowls and pulled vases were made during the 1940s. I may have added fuel to this speculation by noting this theory in my recent publication on opalescent glass. However, I now feel that I must retract this statement, as I have heard from a few readers with verified dates of acquisition of their *IF&F* novelties, all pre-dating the 1920s. However, if any reader of this column knows of actual new production of this pattern in the past 30 years, I would be glad to credit them with any documentable data they provide. I recently was told the table set is being reproduced in emerald green. I hesitate mentioning this undocumented heresay in this column, but if it is true, and one person is saved from wasting his money, it will be worth it.

"Northwood" custard toothpick holders—Maple Leaf, Wild Bouquet and Inverted Fan & Feather patterns.

"ESSEX, MAJESTIC & MASONIC"

MORE AND MORE COLOR DEPARTMENT: I am featuring here three previously undocumented syrups in colors which are not usually considered in these patterns. On the left is Fostoria's ESSEX (No. 1372) in amethyst-flashed crystal, a cheap coloring technique also used by U.S. Glass and sometimes by Northwood. This syrup is worth about $100. In the center is an extremely rare MAJESTIC syrup in emerald green, in which this pattern is seldom found. To date, I have only seen a handled nappy in green Majestic. The pattern dates around 1894-1900, and this syrup would probably bring about $250 in good condition. Majestic is usually found only in crystal and ruby-stained crystal. Finally, I am fortunate to have a picture of the rare ruby-stained MASONIC syrup pitcher mentioned in last month's column. Both Majestic and Masonic were made by McKee before 1900, and both are scarce in color. The value of the ruby-stained Masonic syrup is around $200 in perfect condition.

FIGURAL FEATURETTE

Illustrated here is an extreme rarity in glass animals, a Fenton Elephant "flower bowl." This piece is especially unique in Fenton's Jade Green color shown here. Until my Fenton book was published, many collectors thought this was Cambridge glass. However, this was the No. 1618 flower bowl, appearing in Fenton's 1929 catalogue. This elephant can also be found in crystal, pink, green and a beautiful teal blue. Anyone who owns this rarity in any color can consider themselves most fortunate. The one shown here sold for $200, and possibly was worth more. However they are so scarce that value is difficult to determine.

"FLORETTE"

Featured this month is a water pitcher with every known pattern characteristic of the FLORETTE pattern which was made by the Consolidated Lamp & Glass Company of Ohio and Pennsylvania. Careful study of the above photo reveals the puffed pillow-like sections, much like the tufting on the back of a Victorian Belter couch.

However, the shape of this pitcher is different from the true FLORETTE water pitcher and the color is completely different from anything known made by Consolidated Glass and its brilliant manager Nicholas Kopp. The color is a spattered blend of pink, white and a deep color known today as "tortoise shell".

So here is where I put on my detective's hat and present my own personal theory that this pitcher, which has all the characteristics of glass made around 1885-1890 was the predecessor of the famous FLORETTE pattern. The color of this set leads me to believe it was made by Hopps Glass at the time when Nicholas Kopp was one of its young apprentices, circa 1890. Four years later, when he became manager of the Consolidated factory in Fostoria, Ohio, perhaps he recalled the appealing pillowy pattern made at Hobbs, and designed a complete set very similar to it.

This pitcher is quite scarce. I have only seen two in the past six years. Its value is in the neighborhood of $150. Tumblers would be worth about $35 each.

GLASS ODDITIES

In late 1902 and early 1903, the Perfection Manufacturing company released a line of unusual glass bottles, cruets, syrup jugs and decanters with detachable tops. These items have been seen by myself and others at antique shows with patent markings on the glass or metal parts. These "separating" items made it easier for Victorian housewives to clean the inside of the bottles, as well as simplified the process of filling the syrups and cruets without spillage. One of the advertisements shown here even illustrated this feature. These bottles retailed for 10¢ to 25¢ each and were made in clear glass only. Perfection Manufacturing Company was located in Washington, Pa., and we know very little about this company today.

171

"GLIMPSES OF OLD GLASS"

Featured this month are several pressed glass patterns which, to the best of my knowledge, have never been named or listed in any of the primary glass references of the past thirty years. I have checked the pages of Kamm, Metz and Lee, as well as the less used publications by others, and was unable to locate them anywhere. If I have overlooked them, I would appreciate hearing from my readers who keep close tabs on my mistakes. Rather than hold up this report to check into the patterns further, I am going to present this thumbnail "sketch" for your enjoyment.

All of these unlisted patterns were advertised in the pages of early turn-of-the-century glass company trade journals. Most are dated, but occasionally I failed to note the publication date when I was photostating the copies.

Ad No. 1 appeared in an 1896 issue of *China, Glass & Lamps* and was originally called the MANHATTON pattern of the Tarentum Glass Company of Pennsylvania. Note the spelling of this pattern is different from the spelling of the "Manhattan" pattern made by U.S. Glass circa 1904. This pattern is known only in crystal and according to an early release, Tarentum reported "larger sales than anything the firm has ever gotten out."

Ad No. 2 is from an 1898 trade journal featuring a pattern I am naming LIVERPOOL DIAMOND. It is very similar to other patterns, including "Melrose," combining a motif of diamond and fans. This pattern was made by Specialty Glass Company of East Liverpool, Ohio.

Ad No. 3 was found in an 1899 issue of *Illustrated Glass & Pottery World*, and I am naming it ZIPPERED SPEARPOINT. It was made by the Central Glass Works of Wheeling, W.Va.

Ad No. 4 came from a late 1901 issue of *China, Glass & Pottery Review*, and illustrates a known "Ladders" pattern cruet along with an unidentified spooner. I am calling this new discovery NOTCHED FINECUT. My memory may be playing tricks on me, but I recall owning a spooner in this pattern several years ago in custard glass. The pattern is very similar to Heisey's "Panelled Cane."

Ad No. 5 is only a piece of filler from a 1902 trade journal, but it identifies a pattern I named INVERTED EYE in my book *1,000 Toothpick Holders*. It was the No. 519 pattern of the National Glass Company and is known only in crystal. The manufacturer was not known at the time of publication, so toothpick collectors may want to make a note of this in their books.

Ad No. 6 is from a December 1904 trade journal and attributes a pattern I am naming HORSESHOE COMET. It was made by the Ohio Flint Glass Company of Lancaster, Ohio, and is known only in crystal. It is very similar to "Aztec," "Whirligig" and "Buzz Star," as well as several others. Apparently Haley's Comet had a big influence on the design of patterns at the turn of the century.

Next (Ad No. 7) we have a 1905 advertisement from the Evansville Glass Company of Indiana. This little-known company featured a pattern they called FERNETTE, which I see no reason to change here. It was made only in crystal.

Ad No. 8 apparently dates from 1900-1901 according to the names assigned to the two previously unlisted patterns illustrated. The names TWENTIETH CENTURY and "1901" will suffice for identification of these two designs of the Co-Operative Flint Glass Company of Beaver Falls, Pennsylvania.

AD 9—This was listed in Kamm 6, simply as DIAMOND, so I didn't do much of an injustice calling the pattern DUNKIRK DIAMOND. Kamm shows an ad reprint (the water pitcher) on page 67 of her book so at least my ad reprint is an exclusive for the *Glass Review*. My big mistake on this pattern is estimating the date to be after 1902.

MANHATTON PATTERN—8 in. Straight Nappy.

Ad No. 1

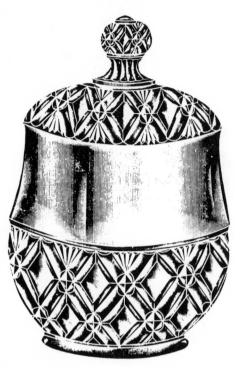

The Specialty Glass Co.,

EAST
LIVERPOOL,
OHIO......

Manufacturers of

FINE
TABLE
WARE
AND SPECIALTIES.

Ad No. 2

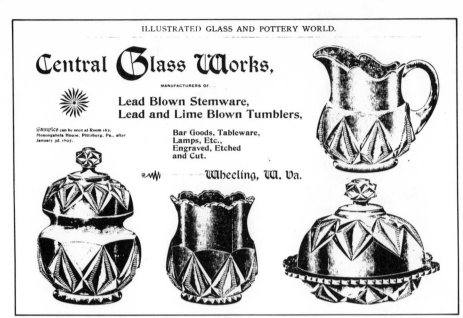

Central Glass Works,

MANUFACTURERS OF. ..

Lead Blown Stemware,
Lead and Lime Blown Tumblers,

Samples can be seen at Room 162,
Monongahela House, Pittsburg, Pa., after
January 3d, 1897.

Bar Goods, Tableware,
Lamps, Etc.,
Engraved, Etched
and Cut.

Wheeling, W. Va.

Ad No. 3

Tarentum Glass Co.

TARENTUM, PA.

GLASS TABLE WARE

In Crystal and Colors, plain
and decorated, in gold and
floral decorations.

Illustrations on application.

:::

New York Sample Rooms :

24 Park Place.

Ad No. 4

Ad No. 5

176

Ohio Flint Glass Company Lancaster Ohio

=== MANUFACTURERS ===

Pressed & Blown Glassware

SAMPLE ROOMS

BOSTON, 144 High St.
NEW YORK, 25 W. Broadway
PHILADELPHIA,
         922-924 Market St.

SAMPLE ROOMS

BALTIMORE, 1 S. Hanover St.
CHICAGO, 45 E. Randolph St.
ST. LOUIS, 404 N. Fourth St.
SAN FRANCISCO, 110 Suter St.

Ad No. 6

Ad No. 7

Ad No. 8

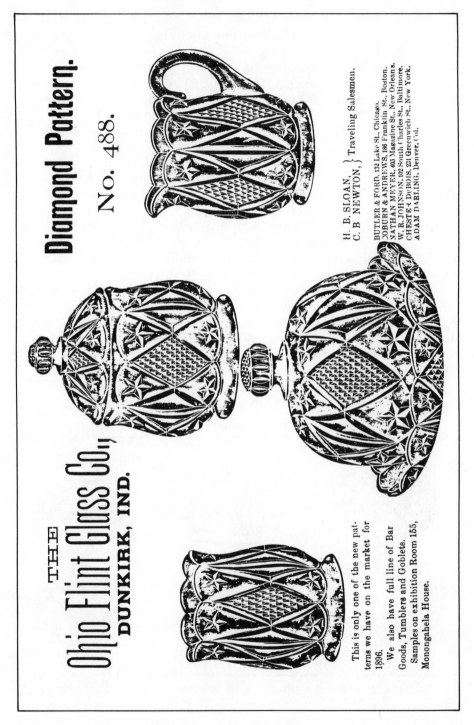

Diamond Pattern.

No. 488.

THE
Ohio Flint Glass Co.,
DUNKIRK, IND.

H. B. SLOAN, } Traveling Salesmen.
C. B NEWTON, }

BUTLER & FORD. 132 Lake St., Chicago.
COBURN & ANDREWS, 186 Franklin St., Boston.
NATHAN MEYER, 405 Magazine St., New Orleans.
W. R. JOHNSON, 102 South Charles St., Baltimore.
CHESTE 4 DuBOIS, 231 Greenwich St., New York.
ADAM DARLING, Denver, Col.

This is only one of the new patterns we have on the market for 1896.

We also have full line of Bar Goods, Tumblers and Goblets. Samples on exhibition Room 155, Monongahela House.

Ad No. 9

179

LET LAMPS
Light Up Your Life

One of the most popular forms of collectible glass is what is known today as the miniature lamp. Early catalogues referred to these as "night lamps" implying that they were used to provide a dim glimmer of light—probably for small children afraid of the dark. These tiny lamps reached the peak of their popularity around 1900, as a wealth of ads which I have found now reveals. As a special bonus to readers of the *Glass Review*, I will be reprinting for the next few issues the vast majority of these early ads.

One of the best reference books on any type of collectible glass is the book *Miniature Lamps* by Frank and Ruth Smith. The pictures are incredibly detailed, the text complete and well prepared, and the layout very professional. However, the Smiths were unable to name the makers of many of their lamps, nor the primary year of production, both of which I will be sharing with you here. I will also be adding small bits of data about these lamps not previously reported.

The companies most responsible for miniature lamp production were Consolidated Lamp and Glass, Coraopolis, Pa., Fostoria Glass Company, Moundsville, W.Va., Gillinder & Sons, Philadelphia, Pa., Eagle Glass & Manufacturing Co., Wellsburg, W.Va., and Dithridge & Company at Pittsburgh. There were others who produced these lamps, but not on the major scale of those listed here.

Since Consolidated apparently led the field in "night lamp" production, I will begin with some of their early ads.

Some of the Consolidated's Trade Makers

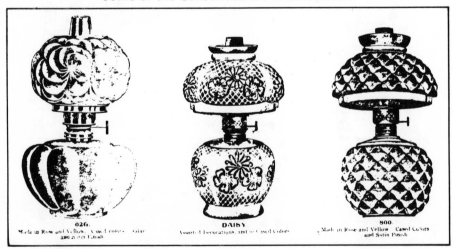

Perhaps the most popular and recognizable pattern made by Consolidated is the COSMOS pattern, which AD No. 1 reveals was originally called "Daisy," referring to the flower in the center, rather than the two at its side. According to the Smiths (No. 286), this lamp appeared in a Westmoreland catalogue for 1890. The ad shown here is from an 1899 trade journal, and seems to be in direct conflict with the earlier attribution. The COSMOS lamp can be found in decorated milk glass and in cased colors of pink and yellow. Cased green or blue would be extremely rare. The lamp is more commonly found in crystal, painted white to simulate milk glass.

AD No. 1 also illustrates a PANSY lamp with a BULGING LOOPS base. This lamp is shown in the Smith book (No. 389), properly attributed. It seems ironic that Consolidated would not make a matching base for this lovely shade. This shade is similar, but not identical, to the PANSY toothpick holder shown in my Book 1. Besides the pink (rose) and yellow cased colors mentioned in the ad, this lamp is also known in blue cased glass, all in shiny or satin finish. Finally we have the CONE lamp, made in the same colors. This is Smith's No. 394 lamp.

| No. 1 Paris
Night Lamp. | No. 2 Paris
Night Lamp. | Daisy
Night Lamp. | No. 02
Night Lamp. |

In the Spring of 1898 another Consolidated Ad again illustrated a COSMOS lamp, but it also revealed a BULGING LOOPS lamp with the matching shade (far right). But far more *important,* AD No. 2 illustrates the two variations of the TORQUAY pattern night lamp. The pattern in these lamps can also be found in a full line of tableware, in colors of opaque white (usually decorated), cobalt blue and pigeon blood. This lamp is found primarily in decorated or plain milk glass and would be very rare in color. It was originally called the "Paris" lamp, and both are shown in Smith (Nos. 188 and 189).

AD No. 3 reveals only a portion of their "Iris" lamp on the left, which is shown in Smith (No. 396) in blue satin glass. It is also known in decorated milk glass and has not previously been attributed. The ad dates from February, 1898. On the right is the "Kitty" night lamp (Smith No. 274), known only in decorated milk glass.

AD No. 4 reveals a decorated lamp which is also known in a rare red satin glass (Smith No. 302 and No. 303). The ad is from a 1900 issue of *China, Glass & Pottery Review* and the lamp has not previously been attributed.

THE LAMP MAKERS OF AMERICA.

A FIRM WHICH MAKES OVER 2,000,000 LAMPS ANNUALLY.

In a recent issue of the trade journals, the Consolidated Lamp & Glass Co. freely concede that "the lamp of the future may be made by others," and express themselves content to make the lamp of the present. A visit to either their salesrooms in New York, Pittsburgh, or their gigantic manufacturing plant in Coroapolis will fully convince the visitor that they not only make the lamps of the present, but they make them in ample quantities, from the tiniest colored gem that glows through the darkness while all the household dreams, to the mammoth and stately banquet, graceful, superb, attractive and artistic, whose center draft duplex burner sheds radiance over feast and festival in courtly halls of luxury, the parlors of leisure, the residences of the cultured, and the millions of homes of the people, whose ensemble constitutes humanity. With

AD No. 5 is not really an ad at all. Actually it is a press release which included an illustration of the PANELLED COSMOS lamp which also was previously unattributed. The story dates around 1900 and extolled the fact that Consolidated made over 600 lamps a day, which is how they came up with the 2 million figure. A portion of this story is reprinted here for your enjoyment.

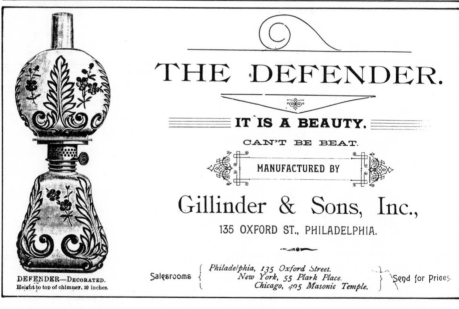

ADS No. 6 and 7 illustrate the "Primrose" and "Defender" lamps, made by Gillinder & Sons of Philadelphia. The Primrose lamp is so rare it isn't even shown in the Smith book. It is shown here in superb detail from an original 1896 advertisement. For more about this company, read last month's column on Gillinder's Easter novelty line.

The Defender lamp is shown in Smith (No. 240) and is known only in decorated milk glass. This ad dates from 1898 and is previously unattributed.

AD No. 8 dates about 1899 and illustrates the unusual handled lamp which Smith calls GOTHIC ARCH. The chimney is original and both base and shade are in milk glass. This lamp (Smith No. 163) is attributed here for the first time. The ad also illustrates a charming salt shaker and a basket full of novelty glass eggs.

The Eagle Glass & Mfg. Co.

The new line of this company, which has been ready for some weeks, can now be seen almost in its entirety at the office of the New York representatives, Doctor & Co., 48 Park Place. It embraces over thirty distinct lines of lamps, and quite an extensive assortment of globes in opal and solid tints. The line has been produced with special regard to moderate prices and will be found particularly strong in this respect, offering good shapes and pretty decorations for very little money. The No. 660, which we illustrate, may be had in three tints, light blue, canary and green being the color tones. Either globes or domes are offered on all the lamps. The two night lamps which we show are new productions, the "Liberty" in red, green or yellow, and the "Juno" in red, blue or yellow. The eagle decoration shown on one will add greatly to its selling qualities at the present time. In the line of globes the decorations consist of prints and gold on the opal and filled-in decorations, with gold, on the solid colors.

AD No. 9 again is a press release with illustrations of their JUNO and LIBERTY night lamps. Both are known only in decorated milk glass, the latter being more popular because of the Americana design. This story appeared in 1898. JUNO is shown in Smith (214) in poorly decorated milk glass. The story here states the lamp was made in red, blue or yellow. However, these colors were fired onto a milk glass blank and were not true colored glass at all. The LIBERTY lamp (Smith No. 275) can be found in several decoration variations.

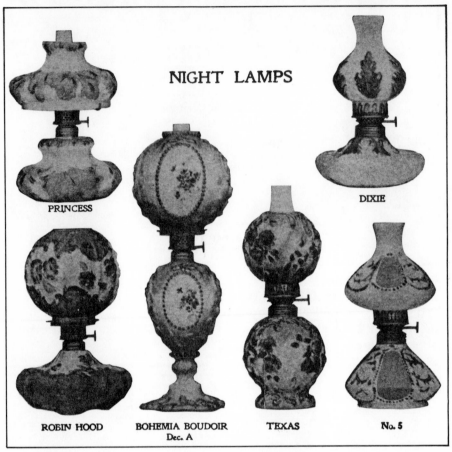

NIGHT LAMPS

PRINCESS

DIXIE

ROBIN HOOD

BOHEMIA BOUDOIR
Dec. A

TEXAS

No. 5

AD 10—Reprinted here is a page from an early Fostoria Glass Company lamp catalogue, dating about 1900. this page features a number of decorated milk glass miniature lamps (night lamps) some of which were also made in colored satin glass.

The PRINCESS lamp is shown in Smith (Figure 107), and has been massively reproduced in many colors by L. G. Wright. The reproductions have rather thick, heavy shades, whereas the old shades are lighter in weight and quite thin around the rim. This lamp can also be found in red satin and pink satin. Collectors today refer to this as the PLUME pattern lamp.

Shown in Smith as Figure 292, the ROBIN HOOD lamp can also be found in red and clear satin glass. Today collectors refer to it as the SPIDER WEB lamp because of a faint, almost invisible web sometimes found in the background of the pattern. To date, it has not been reproduced.

Although the example shown in Smith has no decoration (Figure 307), the catalogue here shows it probably did originally. Quite often the hand painting was poorly fired for permanence, and easily wore off as the years passed. Although this lamp is included on a page with night lamps, the company label leads me to believe it was originally a small boudoir lamp.

I can understand the name for this next lamp if, and only if, the roses are painted yellow—but usually they are not. Shown in Smith as their Figure 201, this TEXAS lamp is found only in decorated milk glass.

Fostoria's No. 5 night lamp is in a pattern which has become known as DRAPED BEADS. A toothpick holder is shown in my first book, and a salt shaker in Peterson's book. The pattern is known only in plain and decorated milk glass, and is shown in Smith as Figure 184.

Finally we have the DIXIE lamp, which as far as I can find, is not pictured in the Smith book on miniature lamps. Many similar lamps are shown, but not this one. None of the five other lamps are attributed in the Smith book either, so this reprint provides the first solid documentation on location and date of manufacture.

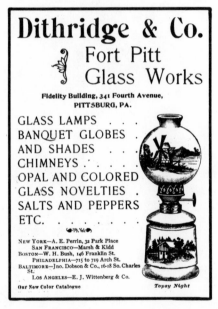

AD 11 reveals a charming little decorated night lamp referred to as the TOPSY, made about 1899 by Dithridge & Company. The lamp with similar decoration is shown in Smith (Figure 339).

A VERY HANDSOME LAMP № 89. MADE IN CARDINAL, AZURE AND
BRAHAM BY THE PITTSBURG LAMP, BRASS & GLASS CO.

In February, 1902 three companies merged to form the Pittsburg Lamp, Brass & Glass Company, and AD 12 appeared shortly thereafter. The lamp shown was not a miniature, but a full size parlor lamp. I am showing it anyway to illustrate the pattern, since the miniature lamp has been reproduced in several colors. Also, I mentioned the rare tumbler found in this pattern in this issue's gossip column. The pattern is known as BEAD AND DRAPE, and is shown in Smith as Figures 400 (an old one) and 403 (a reproduction by L. G. Wright). The shades on the old lamps are thin and light and, in red satin, have an orange cast to them when held up to a bright light.

LAMP WITH STEIN FOR BASE. MADE BY A. J. HALL & CO.
MERIDEN, CONN.

AD No. 13 illustrates a very, very rare "stein lamp" which possibly was stencil decorated as opposed to hand decorated. It is not even shown in Smith's book, so information is somewhat sketchy at this time. The company which made this lamp, A. J. Hall & Company, also made "opal" glass cracker jars and table novelties, as well as full-size lamps. This ad dates from August, 1902.

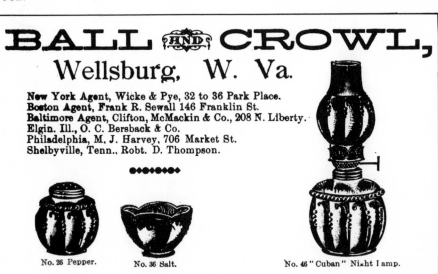

BALL AND CROWL,
Wellsburg, W. Va.

New York Agent, Wicke & Pye, 32 to 36 Park Place.
Boston Agent, Frank R. Sewall 146 Franklin St.
Baltimore Agent, Clifton, McMackin & Co., 208 N. Liberty.
Elgin. Ill., O. C. Bersback & Co.
Philadelphia, M. J. Harvey, 706 Market St.
Shelbyville, Tenn., Robt. D. Thompson.

No. 26 Pepper. No. 36 Salt. No. 46 "Cuban" Night lamp.

I must admit I never heard of Ball & Crowl of Wellsburg, W. Virginia. AD No. 14 appeared around 1900 in an issue of "China, Glass & Lamps," and features a milk glass night lamp which they called their "Cuban" line. This is Smith's Figure 55 example. Note the matching salt shaker. Perhaps other items can be found with this same pattern.

The last three lamps were offered in ads by William R. Noe of New York City. It is my opinion that Mr. Noe was a manufacturer's representative or import agent peddling European-made glassware here in America. All three of the Noe lamps appear to be foreign.

No. 46. Dragon Candle Stick.   Little Beauty Night Lamp.

WE CARRY A FULL LINE OF THESE GOODS

Very
Popular
Lamp

Four colors

Pink
Rose
Green
Amberina

GREAT
SELLERS

Shall we mail you circular of Novelties. etc.?

WM. R. NOE, 33 Park Place, N. Y. City

AD No. 15 appeared in late 1899 and features the Smith No. 439 example, reportedly made in pink (cranberry opal?), rose (plain cranberry), green and amberina. Smith reports a vaseline color as well.

190

AD No. 16 illustrates a satin "Mother-of-Pearl" night lamp which Noe lists made in five colors. However, Smith (Figure 601) lists only pink, green and blue. Makes me curious what the other two colors could be—perhaps yellow and lavender. This ad dates around 1901.

Finally, we wrap up this special report with a beaded pattern which was offered in November, 1900. The ad states "hot from the oven" and calls the lamp their "New Beauty." You will note that the lamp retailed originally for only 25¢, which seems astounding when you consider the same lamp today in cranberry would bring $150-200 easily. The ad only lists three colors, ruby (cranberry), purple and green, but Smith (Figures 367 & 368) shows this lamp in two variations of spatter glass.

Today, miniature lamps represent a very popular form of glass collecting, with prices rising very rapidly. I am seeing lamps sell today for $400 which only two years ago were bringing a mere $200. However, there are many pitfalls in this field. You have to be very careful of reproductions, avoid mismatched shades and bases, learn which lamps are rare and which are common, check for cracks or repairs, and many other facets which will take time to pick up. However, with two superb references now on the market to aid you in this field, I recommend these tiny little "sleepers" (is that another pun?) to anyone susceptible to the charm of the miniature night lamp.

POTOMAC AND 11 INCH GLOBE.

In the January, 1979, issue of *Glass Review,* I featured two Gone-With-The-Wind lamps made by Fostoria Glass Company in 1902. Illustrated here are two more lamps which appeared in the same advertisement. The hand-painted decoration on most of the Fostoria lamps surpassed even the superb artistry found on the lamps of their major competitors — Consolidated Lamp and Glass Co. and Pittsburgh Lamp, Brass & Glass Co.

Today's value of these lamps is based upon several factors — size, colors and present condition. Very few are found today with their original shades, so be careful that the lamp you are buying does not have a repainted shade. The more vibrant the colors, the higher the value. Lamps with portraits of animals bring bigger prices than those with floral decoration. A lamp with Indians painted on it can bring as much as $1,000 today in good condition. A lamp with a repainted shade has about half the value of an original.

The ad reprinted here mentions a line of "basket lamps." I have an original 1900 Fostoria lamp catalog which illustrates nothing looking like a basket, so I am somewhat intrigued to what they are referring. Perhaps one of our readers has a lamp fitting the description above and can share a photograph with us.

BEAUMONT LAMPS

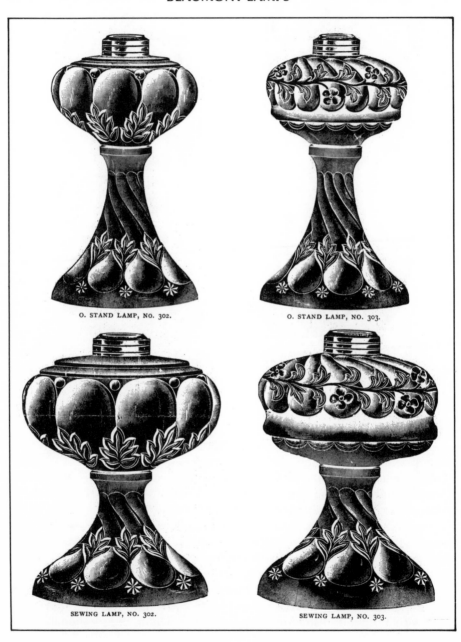

O. STAND LAMP, NO. 302.

O. STAND LAMP, NO. 303.

SEWING LAMP, NO. 302.

SEWING LAMP, NO. 303.

Last month I featured Gone-With-The-Wind lamps in decorated opaque glass. This month I am featuring pressed glass oil lamps in clear glass.

As far as I can ascertain, the lamps shown here in Beaumont's Number 302 and 303 were made only in clear glass and only in the two shapes. Beaumont referred to the taller lamps as "stand lamps" and the shorter lamps as "sewing lamps." This lamp in colored glass would be rare.

This advertisement was taken from an April, 1902, issue of "China, Glass & Pottery Review."

FRY CUT GLASS

WONDERFUL ADVANCEMENT

"THE NEW PIECES OPEN YOUR EYES"

ARTISTIC
and
DEEP CUTTING

PURE
and
BRILLIANT METAL

Electric Lamp at Lewis and Clark Exposition

H. C. Fry Glass Co.

ROCHESTER •• PENNSYLVANIA

Reprinted here is an August, 1905, advertisement illustrating a superior cut glass electric lamp made by the H. C. Fry Glass Company. The cut glass industry was reaching a peak about this time, with more than 185 "cutting shops" in America. According to a 1907 "Glass & Pottery World," many were departments of pressed glass factories where the cutting was done on their own product. Others cut chiefly for large distributors and special chain stores, while a few minor shops supplied product for trading-stamp publishers. This left about fifty factories competing for the general cut glass market, of which H. C. Fry was one of the biggest. Much of their glass can be found today with an acid etched signature, which offers added value.

The lamp shown here is undoubtedly a prime example of their output, as it was featured in their display at the 1905 Lewis and Clark Exposition.

How about this for a basket collector? Handled baskets are especially unique in cut glass, and this one is an especially fine example which was offered by H. C. Fry Glass Company of Rochester, Pa., in 1905. Along with Libbey, Fry led the field in the production of cut crystal in the early twentieth century.

"TWO UNLISTED COLORED CRUETS"

This week I am featuring two previously unlisted colored pattern glass cruets in patterns about which little was known. These two cruets are illustrated here without stoppers, since those which were in them were not original.

The cruet on the left is in a pattern called *Hobnail with Bars*. It is quite short and is in a deep amber color. The cruet on the right is of standard height and is colored a pale vaseline yellow. I call this cruet *King's Block*.

Ruth Webb Lee does list the *Hobnail with Bars* pattern in her book "Victorian Glass", but she illustrates only pieces from the table set. In those pieces, the "bars" cross-hatch each other to form diamonds. In fact, Metz, in her second volume, saw fit to change the name of the pattern to "Hobnail in Big Diamond" without investigating the facts concerning this pattern further.

Lee mentions the fact that the berry bowls of this pattern have vertical bars between the hobs, but she shows no illustration or drawing. In fact, to date I have not seen this variation of the pattern in any publication on pattern glass. The cruet illustrated here was not even listed by Lee, although

196

she did allow for the possibility that other forms existed other than the table set and berry set.

Hobnail with Bars was the No. 307 pattern of Challinor, Taylor & Company, also appearing in an 1891 catalogue of the United States Glass Company (which will be reprinted in my Book 5, soon to be released). It was made primarily in crystal, with limited production in amber and in opalescent white.

The *King's Block* pattern on the right was listed previously only by a number in Revi's book on pressed glass. It was the #312 pattern of the King Glass Company, Pittsburgh, Pa. The pattern also appeared in a wine glass in a 1907 United States Glass Company Catalogue as #4771.

I named the pattern *King's Block* because of its similarity to the *Hobb's Block* pattern. Both of these patterns were reissued by U.S. Glass in 1891.

Since none of the pioneers in glass research had listed *King's Block* before, we can assume that it is quite scarce. I can only guess at the existence of a table set or water set. Only the cruet and wine glass can be documented by this writer at this time. However, since it was made in color, you can rest assured that it is high on my priority list for future detective work.

Care should be taken not to confuse the *Hobnail with Bars* pattern for the similarly named "Barred Hobnail". The pattern shown here has not been reproduced, whereas "Barred Hobnail" has.

Amber cruet in Hobnail with bars and canary cruet in King's Block.

197

"MELON RIBBED"

Recently produced miniature lamp in beautiful pigeon blood color. This "melon ribbed" pattern is very similar to the Bulging Loop miniature lamp for which it is frequently confused. However, the older lamp has an "umbrella" type shade, not a round globe. This lamp also was made in red satin and decorated milk glass. The lamps appeared in a 1975 catalogue of L. G. Wright but possibly were made even earlier than that date.

Reproduction miniature lamp by L.G. Wright.

"MICHIGAN, SADDLE AND COIN"

TOOTHPICK HOLDERS OF THE MONTH: This month I am featuring three especially rare toothpick holders which have been previously documented in other colors but not shown in any of my books in ruby-stained. On the left is the MICHIGAN "state" pattern, known only in crystal and color-stained crystal. It was reproduced in colors. The ruby-stained is the rarest version, and this toothpick is worth about $100. It was made around 1902. In the center is the SADDLE figural toothpick, made in crystal and colors, but again quite rare in ruby-stained. No maker is known, but it dates around 1895-1900 and is worth about $75. Finally on the right is the extremely rare, and quite valuable, COIN or U.S. Coin toothpick holder, made in 1892 for only a short time by U.S. Glass Company, Factory O (Central) and H (Hobbs). It is a massively reproduced toothpick, but not in this color. The example shown here is "rough" but an example in good condition can bring as much as $400. In frosted crystal, an old one is worth only about $125.

MILK GLASS NOVELTIES

One of the most popular forms of collectible glass is the figural or novelty item made in the shape of something natural or lifelike. This month I am featuring a small covered dish in the form of a fainting couch or Victorian day bed. This is a piece of milk glass stained a rusty brown on the pattern to give the piece added dimensions. It is five inches long and two inches wide. This is an extremely rare little Victorian novelty, dating around 1890, which today is worth about $100 to a collector of milk or novelty glass. It was probably meant to hold hair pins originally.

With the Easter season upon us, I thought readers of the *Glass Review* might like seeing an early ad featuring some charming glass novelties for holiday enjoyment. This ad appeared in a January, 1903, issue of the *Crockery and Glass Journal*.

This advertisement features a number of "opal" or milk glass items made by Gillinder & Sons of Philadelphia, Pa. This company should not be confused for the Gillinder & Sons of Greensburg, Pa., which merged into the giant United States Glass Company in 1891. After this merger, James Gillinder opened a glass factory at Philadelphia for the production of lamps, table condiments (syrups, sugar shakers) and novelties. Reportedly, Mr. Gillinder signed an agreement at the time he sold out to U.S. Glass not to produce tablewares for a period of twenty years.

Ironically, James Gillinder died on March 5, 1903, at the age of 58, just after the appearance of this ad. Other publications place his death as late as 1907. The company continued under the management of his three sons, and I believe it is still in business today (as Gillinder Brothers, Inc.).

I would like to take this opportunity to wish all my readers and their families the happiest of Easter greetings.

EASTER COMES ON APRIL 12th, 1903.

HERE ARE SOME NOVELTIES FOR YOU.

No. 4 Egg. Decorated and Gilt.

"Just Out"—Easter.

No. 46. Plate. Decorated

No. 1. Egg Cup.

GILLINDER & SONS,
INCORPORATED,
135 Oxford St., Philadelphia.

Illustrated on the next page is a grouping of milk glass novelties made by Gillinder & Sons of Philadelphia, Pennsylvania. This advertisement appeared in a 1900 issue of the *Crockery and Glass Journal,* a trade magazine for the glass and pottery industries.

All of the items featured were hand-decorated with flowers. The majority of the pieces combined to make up a boudoir set, although there seems to be no matching design amongst them.

Gillinder & Sons originally was located in Pittsburgh before the factory was purchased by the giant U.S. Glass Company merger. Part of the terms of that sale were that Gillinder agreed not to produce tableware for twenty years. The firm relocated and stayed in business manufacturing novelties, jars and lamps. By 1935 all operations for this company were concentrated at their Port Jervis, New York, location. As far as I can tell, they are still in business today.

I am fortunate to have studied a rare U.S. Glass Company catalogue which included a section on Factory G (Gillinder) and it is unfortunate that these brilliant craftsmen were relegated to the production of dime store novelties and canning jars. Some of the early Gillinder patterns which attest to their brilliance include the popular WESTWARD HO, LIBERTY BELL and CLASSIC.

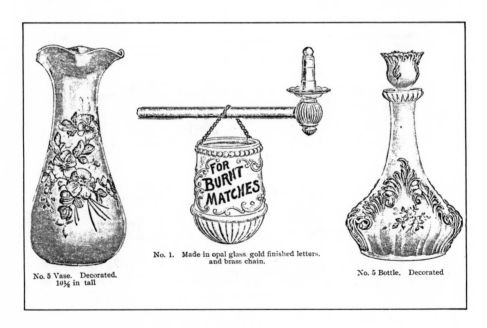

No. 5 Vase. Decorated.
10½ in tall

No. 1. Made in opal glass gold finished letters, and brass chain.

No. 5 Bottle. Decorated

"MOLD-BLOWN OPALESCENT"
TWO UNLISTED PATTERNS

This month I am featuring two different blown opalescent patterns which have never been officially listed in any books, including my own. This is one of the rewards of glass research—discovering pieces of the past and sharing them publicly for the first time.

Actually the glass shown here should be referred to as "mold-blown," since it is blown into a mold to give the piece of glass its general shape and design. There are literally dozens of mold-blown opalescent patterns which were virtually ignored in the early glass references of Kamm, Metz and Lee. For instance, did you realize that the popular Spanish Lace, Daisy & Fern and Seaweed were not even mentioned in those books? Thus, for years this field of glass collecting was shrouded with mystery and confusion, with no reference material available to aid collectors. When the reproduction blown opalescent came out in the 1950's, everyone became immediately suspicious of the good early pieces from the 1890's; and prices remained at rockbottom.

Now that story has changed dramatically. Collectors have new reference material to help them and are aware of the differences between recent and early patterns and shapes.

Pictured first is an extremely rare (only two are known) water pitcher in a pattern I am naming FLORAL EYELET. If a pitcher was made, then there must be a tumbler, although none have been reported to date. The example shown here is from a private collection, but one just like it showed up at a Midwest show for $275. The maker is unknown at this time, but it dates from around 1900 or perhaps even earlier. Only blue opalescent has been reported, although it is likely that it can also be found in white and cranberry opalescent.

Next we have a covered sugar bowl in a pattern I am naming BLOWN OPALESCENT SPIRAL. This is very similar to the ribbed patterns known as "Reverse Swirl" and "Chrysanthemum Base Swirl," but the swirls on this pattern run perpendicular as opposed to angles. I decided to avoid using the ribs in the mold as part of the name in order to prevent confusion for the similar pressed glass pattern "Ribbed Spiral."

This sugar bowl, in blue opalescent, and a tumbler are the only two items I have seen in BLOWN OPALESCENT SPIRAL. However, if there is a sugar bowl, undoubtedly other pieces to the four-piece table setting should also exist somewhere. The maker of this pattern is a matter of speculation at this time, but the mold is identical to the one used on the Ribbed Coinspot sugar which has been attributed to Hobbs by the Oglebay Institute Museum. No water pitcher has been documented to date, so the shape is not known at this time.*

"NAUGHTY GEISHA

My research into twentieth century glassware is still in its infant stages and occasionally I will be featuring items in this category with very little information to back me up.

Illustrated here is a fabulous satin crystal figurine of a scantily draped Oriental looking woman. I personally refer to this figure as the "Naughty Geisha." The quality of the crystal is superb, extremely heavy with a fire you have to see to believe. I was shown this beautiful figurine at the Glass Bash—but no one seemed to know who made it. It has the "look" and quality of Lalique, but I am sure it is not. I saw the same piece in California three weeks later in a grainier satin finish, totally uncharacteristic of Lalique crystal. It was priced at $275. Both pieces showed good age wear at the base.

Our "Naughty Geisha" probably dates from the 1930's and is probably a European import, possibly French. Perhaps one of our readers can help us on this one.

"OPALESCENT"
Recent Opalescent Discoveries

When I published my book on opalescent glassware in 1975, one of the first things I realized was the futility in trying to make the book a "complete" work. As the book was going to press, I was still tracing down leads on dozens of unlisted patterns and shapes. Last year I wrote a feature for the *Antique Trader* on several opalescent novelties which were not included in the book. This month I am presenting here a special feature on several of the latest discoveries in the highly collectible field of opalescent glass.

To start this feature off I begin with a novelty dish which was not included in the *Trader* column, as I only recently learned about its existence. I have named the pattern LINKING RINGS for obvious reasons. The bowl shown here is in a deep blue opalescent color, very much like the English blue, but I am certain this is an American piece of glass. This beautiful dish dates around 1905 and is worth about $35-40.

Photo No. 2 is a small berry dish in yellow opalescent INSIDE RIBBING. The pattern was included in my book but illustrated only in a catalogue reprint. This little known, simple pattern is quite rare in opalescent colors of white, blue and yellow, but this rarity does not necessarily make it valuable. I have seen pictures of the table set. This four-piece set would be worth about $300, whereas a more ornate Northwood opalescent set can bring from $400 to $600. What determines value is demand. The simplicity of INSIDE RIBBING, and the fact that it was made by the Beaumont Glass

Company, do little to enhance its demand among collectors, no matter how rare it is.

The next three patterns are of the mold-blown variety. Photo No. 3 illustrates a tumbler and the lid to a sugar bowl in the RIBBED COINSPOT pattern. This pattern is listed in my book but not illustrated. The ribbed mold used on this Coinspot variant is the same one used on the RIBBED OPAL LATTICE. Any piece of this pattern can be considered rare. Unfortunately, the Coinspot pattern is one of the least desirable among the mold-blown designs. However, since this version is ribbed and somewhat unique, the values are considerably higher than a plain variant. A cranberry pitcher would be worth about $200-250, whereas a plain cranberry Coinspot pitcher will bring around $100.

Photo No. 4 is a cranberry OPALESCENT HONEYCOMB barber bottle. Care should be exercised not to confuse this pattern with OPALESCENT WINDOWS, which has tinier, rounder colored dots. Close inspection of the two patterns reveals that the dots in OPALESCENT HONEYCOMB are eight-sided and not as close together as the dots in WINDOWS. This pattern dates around 1890, and the bottle shown here is worth about $125. It is known only in a water set, cracker jar and this barber bottle.

Photo No. 5 illustrates for the first time a water pitcher and tumbler in the opalescent WIDE STRIPE pattern. At the time I wrote my book I was uncertain who made the pattern, but all indications leaned towards Hobbs, Brockunier. I now know that the vast majority of it was made by the Nickle Plate Glass Company of Fostoria, Ohio. However, the shape of the pitcher shown here is completely different from the water pitcher made by Nickle, so it is possible the pattern was originally made at Hobbs. This case is not unusual, as blown opalescent patterns, such as Coinspot and Opalescent Swirl, were often copied by competing factories. The pitcher and tumbler shown here are in a pale blue opalescent. WIDE STRIPE is known in four differently shaped pitchers, including a small milk or juice pitcher.

The last two items are English in origin, dating around 1885-1890. There are several ways to determine if a piece of opalescent glass is English or American. The easiest way is to check for a registry code or a distinctive trademark. Other than that it is a matter of pattern and color. I list several patterns in my book, but only a sampling.

One item not included is the small quarter-pound covered butter shown in Photo No. 6. It is in a rich yellow opalescent; and I have named the pattern LORDS & LADIES, which is in keeping with the other British sounding names dubbed out in my book. The pattern is very similar to WILLIAM AND MARY, but a close check will reveal several differences. It is interesting to note here that English opalescent glass is seldom found in complete sets, so I doubt that a creamer, sugar bowl or spooner can be located to match this small-sized butter.

Photo No. 7 is a pattern I named RICHELIEU in my book and illustrates a most unusual item in opalescent glass—a large cracker jar. In American pressed opalescent glass, only the WREATH & SHELL pattern can be found in a cracker jar. The one pictured here is heavily opalescent in a light blue color. It is quite rare and worth about $150. Compare this figure to the value of the same cracker jar in WREATH & SHELL, at around $350. Again we witness the case where it is demand, not rarity, which determines the value of opalescent glass.

Photo No. 1

Photo No. 2

Photo No. 3

Photo No. 4

Photo No. 6.

Photo No. 7

Photo No. 5

UNLISTED OPALESCENT GLASS NOVELTIES

For the past several years I have been offering readers of *The Antique Trader* my columns on pattern glass, but this will be my first cover feature. I have picked this particular subject for two reasons. First, the topic is opalescent glass novelties and these don't fit particularly well into a column on pattern glass. Second, in the past four years since my opalescent glass book was published, a considerable amount of information has come to light which needs to be documented. I do not have immediate plans for another book on opalescent glass, so I will be sharing much of what is newly discovered in this story.

The reason I am so insistent on referring to these featured pieces as "novelties" is that their original purpose was to perform some function in the home considered entirely novel or superfluous. I cannot categorize them as pattern glass, although some do carry "pattern" names. That terminology should be restricted to glass items which were part of an entire table setting of some form. Most of these novelties are a single item, although you will often find the same mold pulled, twisted, ruffled, flattened or flared into a dozen different shapes or more.

The items featured in this story have been photographed with varying degrees of quality over the past four years. I apologize for the poor detail on three of the items, but they are so rare that they were unavailable for reshooting when a better photographer was found. Rather than leave them out of the column altogether, I will take my chances on reproductive quality and include them anyway.

PHOTO A—THE NORTHWOOD SHELL VASE AND FISH-IN-THE-SEA VASE

The rare Northwood Shell tableware pattern is well-known among opalescent glass enthusiasts, but pictured here is the very rare vase in a slight variation of the pattern. At first you might suspect that this was a spooner mold stretched into a vase, but this is not the case. There are a few minute pattern details missing from this vase which are found on the table items. However, the patterns are almost identical, obviously from the same manufacturer, so I will not attempt to change the name and cause confusion. The vase shown here is in a green opalescent.

Also pictured is a green opalescent FISH-IN-THE-SEA vase which has been flared only slightly at the top. Most of these rare vases are found with the upper portion of the vase stretched to 10" or more, which tends to restrict the detail of the upper pattern. This unique vase has all the characteristics of Northwood, although this cannot be confirmed.

PHOTO B—SUNK HONEYCOMB NOVELTY BOWL

This canary opalescent bowl really had me baffled. It is in a known McKee pattern, but this company is rarely credited with opalescent glass production. A caster set is shown in my Book 2, called "Curtain Call", which has original stoppers also identical to the SUNK HONEYCOMB pattern. I only had the loan of this bowl for a short period of time and did not have the opportunity to compare the 21-rayed star base to an actual berry bowl in this pattern. Needless to say, this bowl is quite rare.

PHOTO C—BEADED MOONS AND STARS BOWL

At first glance, this appears to be the BEADED STARS pattern shown in my Book 2 (Figure 424). But a quick check will reveal the two patterns are only similar. The stars on the bowl shown here are only five beads deep, whereas the stars on the BEADED STARS pattern are six beads deep. Also note the tiny "moons" surrounded with beads shown here, a feature entirely missing on the previously listed version. The bowl here is in blue opalescent, and probably had the same origins as BEADED STARS, although the actual manufacturer can only be guessed at this time.

PHOTO D—WIDE PANEL EPERGNE

Although an epergne very similar to this has been documented in carnival glass colors, this variant of the WIDE PANEL EPERGNE has not been listed in opalescent colors. It is known in white and blue and is shown here in green opalescent. The difference between the opalescent and carnival versions is in the base. The one shown here has three distinct receptacles into which the jack-in-the-pulpit lily vases are placed. It is my opinion that this version proved expensive, so the mold was reworked so that the top of the base was one solid piece of glass with holes in the top. This simpler mold was used on the carnival glass production around 1910. A green carnival epergne was offered in a Butler Brothers catalogue that year at the wholesale price of $1.35 each. Credit for both of these variants of the same epergne can be given to Northwood at his Wheeling location.

PHOTO E—RAYED HEART COMPOTE

This little jelly compote is in a pattern reportedly made by the Dominion Glass Company of Toronto, Canada. It is known in crystal in a considerable table service, but only this compote has been reported in opalescent glass. Shown here in blue opalescent, it is illustrated in the Unitt's "Treasury of Canadian Glass" in green opalescent. Dominion had some association with the Jefferson Glass Company in West Virginia, and often you will see known Jefferson patterns referred to as Canadian glass. It is not my position to comment here upon the merits of some of the techniques Canadians have used to determine whether certain patterns are Canadian or American, but I feel that this compote has the look and feel of American glass, circa 1910.

PHOTO F—THE SQUIRREL & ACORN DISH

I refer to this scarce vase simply as a dish since the same mold has been seen flattened and crimped into a novelty bowl and pulled high into a vase. This one is rather in-between. It is shown here in green opalescent and is quite rare in blue opalescent. Undoubtedly white was also made.

PHOTO G—THE LITTLE SWAN NOVELTIES

Only a touch of opalescence can be found on the LITTLE SWAN shown here. This novelty has been well-documented in carnival glass and Depression glass colors, and is even included in my Fenton Book. However, the opalescent version is undoubtedly Northwood's. The blue example shown here has traces of goofus red and gold decoration remaining around the head and neck of the bird. I have also seen this swan in a rich yellow and green opalescent. The Northwood mold was also used by Fenton after 1920, but I doubt Fenton was responsible for opalescent production. Westmoreland and Fenton both made a similar LITTLE SWAN, but there were differences in the molds. Since I am concerned with opalescent glass only in this feature, I will make no attempt to detail the differences. BEWARE OF REPRODUCTIONS!

PHOTO H—THE SURF SPRAY PICKLE DISH

This is the Jefferson Glass Company's #253 pickle which I have named SURF SPRAY because of the similarity to Jefferson's SEA SPRAY olive dish. It is shown here in green opalescent, but is also known in white and blue opalescent. No other matching pieces are known in this pattern which dates from 1906.

PHOTO I—THE DAISY MAY BON-BON

I couldn't think of a more appropriate name for this unusual little handled bon-bon, which has a single leaf-framed daisy in the base. It is shown here in green opalescent, but undoubtedly came in other colors. No maker is known, but it is similar to others known made by Dugan Glass at Indiana, Pennsylvania. DAISY MAY dates about 1910.

PHOTO J—THE JEFFERSON SHIELD BOWL

Named by Hartung in her earlier reference on opalescent glass, no photograph has been offered to date in either her book or mine. It is quite rare and the blue one shown here is only the second one I have ever seen. It is unusual to find it with the pattern detail so intricate. Usually the shields are almost unrecognizable by the time the glass piece has been crimped and refired to obtain the opalescent effect. This was Jefferson's #262 novelty, also dating about 1906.

PHOTO K—THE WILTED FLOWERS BOWL

I apologize for the name of this pattern, but every time I see this piece in a show or flea market, I am amazed by the limited amount of mold-work which went into designing this pattern. This gives the flowers and leaves a weak "wilted" look. Shown here in green opalescent, the bowl has also been seen in blue and white. The "ribbon candy" crimped edge is a characteristic of many Fenton carnival pieces, but this attribution would be inconclusive. It dates about 1908.

PHOTO L—THE MAY BASKET

This was one of those inexplicable oversights during production of my Book 2. This little novelty basket is not especially rare, but I failed to borrow it every time I was visiting with the many collectors who participated in my book. I simply forgot to include it. Since a photograph is not included in the Hartung book either, I am offering one here for your enjoyment. This was Jefferson's #87, made in white, blue and green opalescent.

PHOTO M—THE OLD MAN WINTER BASKET

The smaller version of this basket is included in my book (Figure 210), but the larger basket was not and is shown here. The small basket has no feet, whereas the large one has four stump-like feet. I named this pattern OLD MAN WINTER because I was told that the patent date on the bottom of this basket (I failed to write it down and cannot offer it here) coincides with the year Admiral Byrd discovered the North Pole. Also if you look hard enough you can almost make out the frigid, icey image of a bearded old man. This was Jefferson's #91 pattern, dating from 1906, in the usual colors.

PHOTO N — THE PLAIN PANEL VASE

This vase looks to me as if it was made from the same mold used on the FEATHERS pattern vase, with wide plain panels where the feathers would normally have appeared. The bases on both vases are the same. However, no Northwood trademark can be found in the example shown here, which is usually the case with FEATHERS. The PLAIN PANELS vase dates about 1908, and probably underwent limited production.

PHOTO O — THE UNLISTED OPALESCENT VASES

These vases were grouped together for the photograph, so I will group them together here. The one on the left should be referred to as the OPAL HONEYCOMB VASE, since it is found only in opalescent glass and usually in some form of vase. A bowl would be rare. The tall vase in the middle should be known as the TINY TEARS vase, available in the usual colors. Finally on the right is the RIB & BIG THUMBPRINTS vase, with rather indistinct opalescent thumbprints which would fade even more on a taller vase. No maker can be confirmed on any of the above at this time, but all three date from 1905-1910.

PHOTO A

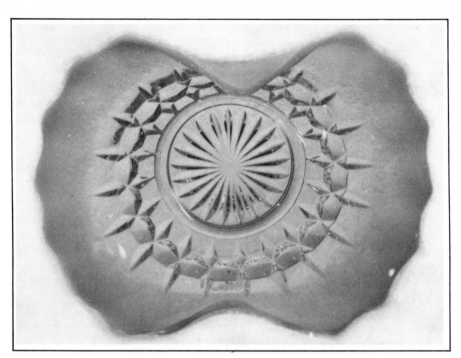

PHOTO B

PHOTO C

PHOTO D

PHOTO E

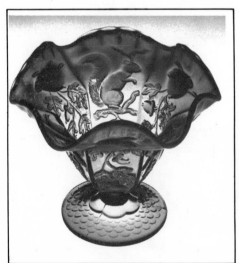

PHOTO F

PHOTO G

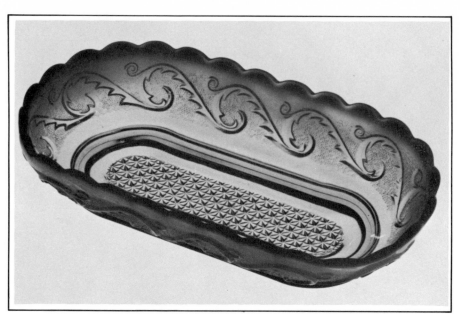

PHOTO H

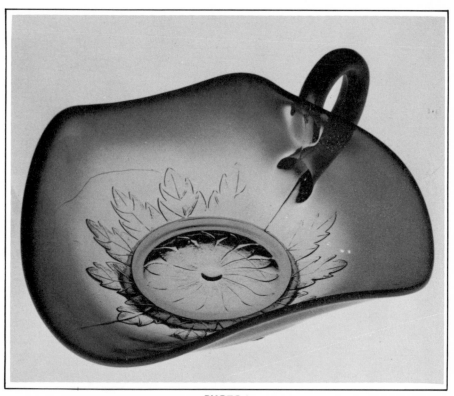

PHOTO I

PHOTO J

PHOTO K

218

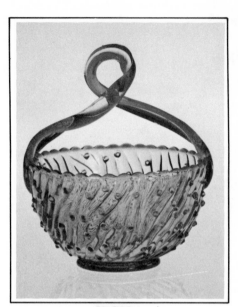

PHOTO L

PHOTO M

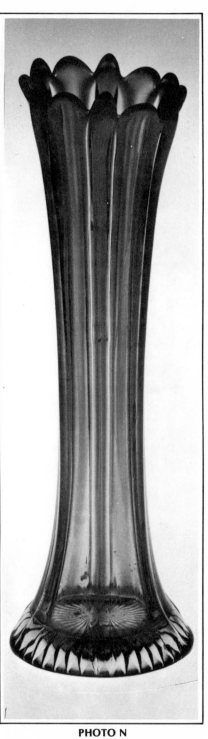

PHOTO N

219

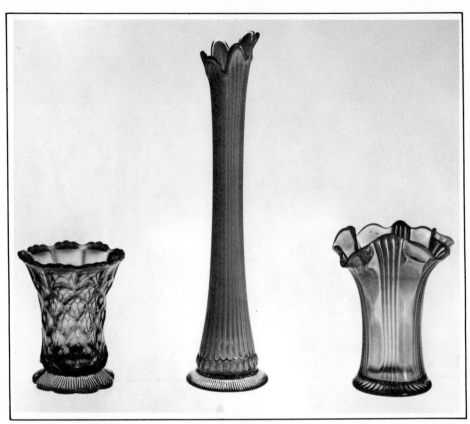

PHOTO O

"PEACOCK BOOKEND

FIGURAL FEATURETTE: Illustrated here is a choice addition to any glass collector's "menagerie." On the right is a 5¾" tall PEACOCK BOOKEND made by Fenton around 1934 in crystal, frosted crystal, frosted Rose pink and frosted green shown here. It is not shown in any of the animal books but is pictured in Weatherman II. Shown next to the "mother" is an adorable miniature version of the Fenton Bookend which matches exactly in every mold detail. I showed this little peacock "chick" to Frank Fenton and asked if he felt it was also made by his company. He checked old inventory records and came up with no record of such an item in the line, so this little fella will remain something of a mystery for now. However, the two make an attractive pair. In fact, an avid glass animal collector could have some fun trying to put together a little family of the peacocks, much like the Hens and Chicks or Pigs and Piglets made by both Heisey and New Martinsville. The value of the large peacock is about $35 in clear, $65 in color. The little peacock, with its attribution a matter of speculation at this point, is worth about $25. It is known only in clear glass.

IS IT POMONA?

I received two letters in the past few months, both of which request information about water pitchers thought to be POMONA ware. For those readers not familiar with this unique form of art glass, I will offer a brief explanation. The process was patented by the New England Glass Company in 1885. There are two types of POMONA, known as First Grind and Second Grind. First Grind involved very expensive intricate hand-carved workmanship. Second Grind was a less expensive method where the blank glass was "rolled" in acid-resistant particles which gave the effect of hand-carving. Neither process was used to any extent after the New England Glass Company closed in 1888.

The first letter is from Jack Roads, Sacramento, CA who enclosed this first photo and asks "I was told this pitcher is POMONA, but can you tell me more about it?"

Actually, the answer to that question is not clear cut. In fact, a toothpick holder in the same exact pattern of "Fish and Seaweed" is shown in Mark Boultinghouses's book on toothpick holders and he calls it PSEUDO-POMONA. He stated that there was considerable controversy about whether this ware can legitimately be included in the POMONA family, since the pattern is molded into the glass. The patterns found in actual POMONA glass is the portion which is left plain of the intricate carving.

However, I can tell you that this unique "Fish and Seaweed" POMONA-TYPE glass is quite rare. I have only seen one toothpick in all my years of collecting and your water pitcher is the first example I've heard of. The applied handle on the pitcher indicates this pattern dates about 1885-1890. I also know of a celery vase and a water bottle in this pattern. It is usually color-stained with amethyst and amber, an obvious copy of the colors used on the ture POMONA. These colors usually faded from usage over the years.

The second letter from Lee and Marva Briix of Hennessey, OK included photo at left, and a request for more information about their water pitcher. They were aware of the fact that the pattern was called FLOWER AND PLEAT in my Book 1. No maker is known, but I did state that this type of glass is often referred to as MIDWESTERN POMONA. This name is used on glass which combines all the effect of ture Pomona, with the frosty combination of clear and acid-coated glass, amber and amethyst staining, and yet there is no intricate hand-carved look to it.

However, the Briix's were confused by the price guide listings of Pomona glass with a "Cornflower" design, and by an article which they read which listed this pitcher as a "scarce Pomona decorated with a passion flower".

I hate to burst anyone's bubble, but FLOWER AND PLEAT is nothing more than frosted and color-stained pattern glass. It is mold-blown, which makes it light in weight, but it does not have nearly the rarity or the value of POMONA glass. It dates about 1895, and can also be found in ruby-stained crystal. I have seen many water pitchers in this pattern over the years, varying in price from $45 to $125. The high prices listed in the guides for the cornflower designed POMONA are for pieces of true POMONA. These prices have nothing to do with FLOWER AND PLEAT, no matter what any dealer tries to tell you.

A final quick reply for Mariana Cox of Anthony, KS. She writes, "I have a 'Lion' pattern lamp exactly like the one in Lee's *Early American Pressed Glass,* plate 90, except the Lion's heads on mine are clear, not frosted. Does this make it more or less valuable?"

I would have to say somewhat less, but not much. The advanced collectors of this pattern prefer to have their sets match, and since most of the Lion pattern was made with frosted lions, I feel they would prefer a matching lamp. However, this lamp is so scarce today that I feel few collectors would quibble about a lack of frosting. I am afraid that I can only estimate the value of this lamp, since I have not seen one for sale. A rough guess would be $220-300, depending upon condition.*

"PONY BOWL"

This month I am featuring the popular PONY bowl in a most unusual light green "stretch" glass. This same bowl is found in carnival colors of marigold and amethyst, but the color shown here is the rarest. This PONY bowl has often been attributed to Northwood, but it is my belief that the pattern was made by the Dugan Glass Company of Indiana, PA. The name of this firm was changed in 1912 to the Diamond Glass-Ware Company after Mr. Dugan left the firm. Since stretch glass was not produced in major quantities until the 1920's, then credit for the bowl shown here technically should go to Diamond. I have shards in this lovely ice green stretch which match the bowl exactly. Unfortunately, three different companies operated at that same factory site where these shards were unearthed. Thus, naming the actual manufacturer must remain a matter of theory and conjecture.

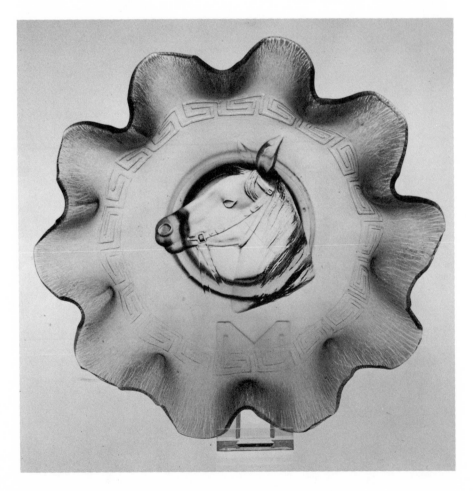

Recent diggings at the Indiana, Pa. factory site unearthed several shards in this pattern.

"STRONG BOX"

Have you ever loved a piece of glass so much you wanted to lock it up for safe keeping? Well, here's an unusual twist on that theme—a glass safe. This little "strong box" is about 6½" tall and possibly was originally designed as a cigar holder. The top lifts off, which is unusual since there is no finial. If there was a finial, I would suspect this unique novelty was designed as a jam jar or pickle holder. However the obviously masculine design, and the "Daisy & Button" design in the glass (sharp enough on which to strike a match), lend credence to the cigar—or cigarette holder theory. The glass is a rich color of amber, and this safe probably can also be found in crystal and blue. This Victorian novelty dates from the 1890's and is quite rare. Value—about $75 in mint condition.

WINE SETS—
Courtesy of the U.S. Glass Co.

This week I will be featuring a number of previously unlisted patterns which have remained something of a mystery among collectors for many years. This is perhaps due to the fact that these patterns were primarily produced (with minor exceptions) only in the wine sets illustrated here. Most of the early pattern books concentrated their attention to goblets (Millard, Metz) pitchers (Kamm) and table sets (Lee). Thus these great glass pioneers overlooked listing, or naming, the patterns shown here—with one exception.

That exception is the Figure C wine set, which Metz named "Tiny Finecut" in her second volume. She correctly lists the set in crystal and emerald green, but failed to list the ruby-stained version (Fig. E, far right). She lists a goblet in this pattern, which I doubt exists. This set was originally called the "Parisian" pattern in an undated U.S. Glass Company catalogue, circa 1910. Metz dates the pattern from the 1890s, but I can find no record of this set in the catalogues prior to 1900. The emerald green set in this pattern sometimes has a stencilled Goddess-like figure on the decanter and tiny cupids eating grapes on the wines.

The Figure A and B wine sets remain unlisted to date, although a large handled decanter in Fig. A is shown on the back of Barrett's book on ruby-stained glass (among unidentified patterns). I am naming this pattern "PEAS AND PODS" for obvious reasons. The set appeared in an 1891 U.S. Glass catalogue, with production at their Factory B—Bryce Brothers, Pittsburgh, Pa. Only the two decanters (with or without handle) and the wine glass have been documented in *Peas and pods* to date.

The Figure B set (U.S. #5601) I am naming "MIRROR AND FAN." This set also was made by Bryce Brothers, circa 1891, but production was continued for some time. This set appeared in a 1910 Butler Brothers catalogue, in gold-decorated green or crystal, for the wholesale price of 87¢ per set. However, this later production reveals a slight difference in the mold of the wine glass. Note that the earlier production includes a row of fans above and below the mirrors, whereas the Figure E (center) wine lacks the fans at the top—as do the wines appearing in the Butler Brothers catalogue. *Mirror and Fan* was also made in a tiny toy-size decanter (only 8½ inches tall) which was advertised in the same wholesale catalogue. As mentioned before, the pattern was made in crystal, emerald green and in ruby-stained.

I know very little about the "VENETIAN" wine set (Figure D), since the catalogue lists it in crystal only, and my research the past few years has been somewhat limited to the colored glass field. It appeared in the undated U.S. Glass catalogue (circa 1910), and I can find no record of a previous listing anywhere.

Among all the different types of glass collectors, I find they fall into three distinct categories: those who collect glass by color or style (carnival, opalescent, ruby-stain); those who collect by maker (Greentown, Northwood,

Sandwich), and finally those who collect by shape or item (toothpicks, goblets, salt shakers, miniatures, spooners, figurals or novelties, table sets, water sets, etc.) Whereas there has been considerable bravura and attention paid to those listed in the final category, the wine glass collectors have been virtually ignored. No publication devoted to the subject has appeared on the market to date, and thus prices on these delicate pieces of glass have remained stable over the past decade. There are few wine reproductions on the market today, unlike the overwrought goblet collector's dilemma. Thus I highly recommend this field to new collectors interested in getting into a relatively inexpensive and safe glass category. A wine glass combines all the charm of a goblet into the relative size of a toothpick holder, making it ideal for collectors with space limitations.

FIGURE A & B—Reprint of 1891 U.S. Glass catalogue illustrating wine sets in the "PEAS AND PODS" and "MIRROR AND FAN" patterns.

Parisian Wine Set.

Venetian Wine Set, Crystal.

FIGURE C—Wine set in the "TINY FINECUT" pattern, reprinted from a U.S. Glass catalogue, circa 1910.

FIGURE D—Reprint from U.S. Glass catalogue, circa 1910, showing their "VENETIAN" wine set.

FIGURE E—Three ruby-stained U.S. Glass wines—Left to Right: "Peas & Pods," "Mirror & Fan," and "Tiny Finecut".

INDEX